MANAGING IN REVERSE

The 8 Steps to Optimizing Performance for Leaders

Jonathan J. Clark

Founder of Kodiak Cakes

MANAGING IN REVERSE

The 8 Steps to Optimizing Performance for Leaders

Print ISBN: 978-1-66788-662-6
eBook ISBN: 978-1-66788-663-3

Printed in the United States of America

Kodiak Bear Publishing, LLC

www.managinginreverse.com

Edited by Elizabeth Hokanson

FOR LEADERS

CONTENTS

PREFACE

The Two Prongs of Leadership

This book was written for you, a leader. And as a leader, you are primarily in charge of two things: objectives and execution.

- By objectives, I mean direction. This is where leaders establish the ambitions, vision, strategy, goals, mission, and values of what they want to pursue and accomplish. This is the first prong of leadership.

- By execution, I mean performance. This is where leaders design and manage the performance engine, or operation, that will achieve their objectives. This is the second prong of leadership.

In developing objectives, visionary leaders are forward-thinking as they look into the future to determine what new outcomes and aspirations they can achieve. Scientists, physicians, explorers, athletes, organizational leaders, and leaders of countries will set objectives that take them into uncharted territories in order to innovate, revolutionize, and accomplish things never done before. In developing well-intentioned, worthy objectives, leaders first carefully examine the environment, including competitive, regulatory, political, economic, and social factors. They also study the potential risks and obstacles. And they examine the requirements and necessary resources, as well as their strengths and weaknesses, before finalizing their purposes.

As leaders assess these various elements, they commonly seek the expertise and counsel of others. Think of the various disciplines that are employed by the leader of a country. The president of the United States, for instance, uses a cabinet of advisors composed of the vice president and fifteen other department executives to develop political objectives. A college football head coach uses a panel of coaching staff to assist him with an upcoming game strategy. A corporate CEO uses her leadership team, board members, and often external consultants to establish business objectives.

Once the right objectives are set, wise leaders also recognize that their objectives can change as new conditions, threats, and opportunities arise. This ability to continuously monitor the environment, adapt, and appropriately alter objectives is what I call "managing forward." Great leaders vigilantly "manage forward."

As objectives are established and reestablished when necessary, leaders must then execute. This is the performance prong of leadership. Here, leaders design and manage the performance engine, or the operation, that will accomplish their objectives. This book instructs leaders how to optimize performance so that objectives are achieved. In this book, you will see that optimizing performance always starts with the end in mind. That focus never changes. This ensures that operations and their outcomes are always aligned with current objectives. In this manner, operations are managed in a back-to-front manner—in reverse order—beginning with the outcomes of an operation and ending with the inputs of an operation. Every operational component between these two points must be properly managed so that optimal performance is incessant. I call this "managing in reverse."

When leaders need to improve performance, they will often outsource this task to external consultants or assign the work to internal teams. Some leaders opt to do the work themselves. Other leaders don't know where to begin and allow mediocre, even poor, performance to perpetuate. Regardless of how a leader chooses to tackle performance issues, it is imperative that they know the proper step-by-step method for optimizing performance.

This knowledge will help leaders more effectively manage external consultants. It will also show leaders how to better direct internal teams who have been assembled to optimize performance. And it will teach leaders how they can individually optimize the performance of their operations in the most holistic and effective way possible.

Through my career, I have observed that many leaders, professionals, and teams struggle to know exactly how to optimize performance. Let me give you two examples.

Example 1, a single operation: Many years ago, I was hired as a consultant by one of the nation's top quality medical centers to help improve their patient flow and bed management processes. Because the hospital had a long history of high occupancy rates, beds were often full of patients. Ironically, this was both beneficial and problematic for the hospital and the community.

On one hand, high patient volumes meant lots of patients were getting treated. Financially speaking, high patient volumes meant the hospital was generating strong revenue. On the other hand, full beds were creating patient flow gridlock, which obstructed patient movement. In fact, it literally prevented new patients from being admitted to the hospital.

For instance, when patient flow gridlock occurred, the emergency and trauma departments went on diversion and routed new patients to other hospitals; inpatient surgical cases were cancelled because there were no beds for post-surgery recovery; interhospital transfers—acute and specialty care patients needing to be transferred to the hospital from other hospitals—were denied; and direct admits from physician offices were also refused. Gridlock also caused internal problems as well. Interdepartmental patient transfers were delayed, where patients needed to be moved from one floor or unit to another. The problem was significant.

In response to the problem, the hospital assembled a large committee to recommend and implement solutions. The committee was composed of its leading physician faculty and administrators from both the hospital and the school of medicine, senior nursing leadership, and key department directors. At the time I was hired, the committee had already been meeting for a couple of months, working to improve patient flow and bed management. During the first committee meeting I attended, I found that the committee had been implementing ideas to fix the complex problem and was brainstorming additional ways to improve patient flow and throughput. I recognized that some of their ideas were on point; others, however, were not.

This committee was falling prey to the same trap that so many do when confronting performance challenges. Although the members of this committee were brilliant, well-trained leaders, they did not know the correct approach for fixing the problem. What the committee needed was not more scholarship and sophistication, but the correct methodology for taking them through the project. After defining the missing steps and backing up the team's momentum enough to implement them, the project became successful. In fact, the hospital was soon recognized as a best practice site for patient flow and bed management.

Example 2, an entire organization: Not many months after the patient flow project, the same medical center assigned me to help with a much larger project—a massive, system-wide performance improvement project. Some organizations would call this a "turn-around" or "transformation" initiative. However, since the hospital was not operating in the red, we mildly called it a "performance improvement" project. The goal of this project was to improve the institution's profitability to help fund the construction of a new hospital and outpatient clinics while simultaneously improving its financial and competitive viability.

As in the case of the patient flow project, the hospital had already assembled an impressive committee composed of its most seasoned leaders to determine how to reduce costs and increase revenue. When I arrived a couple of months after the committee had begun meeting, I realized they were following the same pattern as the patient flow committee. Again, they were trying to solve the problem without knowing the right approach and methodology to guide them through the process. After they adopted the proper approach, the project took a significant turn and became highly successful, adding millions of dollars to the bottom line. In fact, the health system realized its most profitable years to date.

Over the past decades as a high-level operations improvement leader and consultant for some of the finest organizations in the United States, I have observed numerous like cases in which, highly trained and talented leaders, managers, consultants, professionals, and task teams were responsible for optimizing performance but lacked the proper approach to guide them through the process. Commonly, these professionals would meet to brainstorm ideas to address the problems they faced. As they did, I noticed that some task teams brainstormed for ideas that only focused on improving processes through automating workflows or implementing new technology and state-of-the-art systems, equipment, and facilities. Their goal was to increase speed, volume, and efficiency. However, they would leave out critical human components such as leadership, staff, organizational structure, and culture. Other teams seemed to focus their attention on cost and waste reduction, when more could have been accomplished. Still others concentrated on improving quality, customer experience, or safety—again at the expense of other vital opportunities. Some teams had no plan. The purpose of Managing in Reverse is to provide leaders with the definitive approach to achieving optimal performance.

INTRODUCTION

Managing in Reverse

As discussed in the Preface, leaders are essentially in charge of two things: objectives and execution. Said another way, leaders set the direction and are responsible for the optimal performance of operations. At the highest level of organizational leadership, a leader oversees an entire organization, which is simply an operation on a grand scale. Leaders also manage suboperations within an organization, such as divisions, business units, or departments. Professional individuals also manage operations and become leaders in their own fields, such as a surgeon carefully performing heart surgery, or a professional athlete tightly executing his or her sporting event.

Take, for instance, Shaun White in the world of winter sports. He and snowboarding have become synonymous terms. When many people think of snowboarding, they think of Shaun White, "*The Flying Tomato!*" As a five-time Olympian, a three-time Olympic gold medalist, and a thirteen-time Winter X Games gold medalist, he rebranded the sport. Shaun pushed the limits of snowboarding so high that he is often regarded as the world leader who revolutionized the sport as we know it today.

Shaun's superpipe and halfpipe performances were quintessential, as he outclassed other competitors in skill, speed, style, and air. His scores proved it. In the 2010 Vancouver Winter Olympic Games, Shaun earned the highest halfpipe score ever recorded to that time—a 48.4 out of 50 possible points. In 2012, he also became the first person in history to score a perfect 100 points in the superpipe at the winter X Games in Aspen, Colorado.

One of Shaun's trademarks, which helped him rack up points, was his ability to maximize his vertical height, or "amplitude," after "dropping in" on the superpipe or halfpipe with unusual speed. In 2010, at the winter X Games, he flew to a height of twenty-three feet in the air, a new record.

So, as a leader, how do you maximize "amplitude," or the height and performance of your operation, in order to achieve the objectives? Where do you begin? What exactly do you do during each stage of the improvement process to achieve the very best outcomes? *Managing in Reverse: The 8 Steps to Optimizing Performance for Leaders* outlines the precise methodology for achieving the highest performance possible. These successive steps and subtasks take you through an operation in reverse order, managing every component in a succinct, proven way.

As we begin this process, I want to quickly provide you with an overview of the *Managing in Reverse* methodology. In doing so, it is important to note that *Managing in Reverse* is designed to be comprehensive, as it optimizes all aspects of an operation. They include:

- The outcomes of an operation,

- The tangible, nonhuman components of an operation (e.g., systems, processes, equipment),

- The intangible, human components of an operation (e.g., leadership, organizational structure, culture),

- The inputs of an operation (e.g., raw materials, customers, information).

In the chapters of this book, I will explain how these components, as well as other factors, are assessed and optimized according to eight steps and their related tactics. These steps are designed to be succinct and as efficient as possible to implement. It is also important to note that they can be universally applied to any organization or operation in any industry.

Whether a single operation requires improvement (as illustrated in Example 1 of the Preface) or the performance of an entire organization needs transformation (as illustrated in Example 2 of the Preface), the approach for optimizing performance is the same. This is because improving performance involves improving operations. And because the anatomy and function of an operation are the same, regardless of its industry, size, complexity, or type, improving any kind of operation involves the same approach.

So, how does it work? *Managing in Reverse* is based on first examining the current outcomes of an operation prior to considering any improvements. After outcomes are assessed and measured, they are compared against the overall objectives to determine if a gap or an opportunity for improvement exists. You then move backward from the outcomes to the operation itself, and then to the inputs. Working through the remaining sequential steps ensures that the best solutions are identified, implemented, and refined to achieve optimal results. The eight steps are divided into two separate phases: Phase I: Assessment, and Phase II: Implementation, outlined as follows:

PHASE I: ASSESSMENT

Step 1: Measure current performance

Step 2: Establish performance targets

Step 3: Evaluate underperforming operations

Step 4: Benchmark best practice operations

PHASE II: IMPLEMENTATION

Step 5: Recommend operational improvements

Step 6: Implement recommendations

Step 7: Monitor outcomes

Step 8: Refine improvements

Typically, though this will vary based upon each improvement project, *Managing in Reverse* employs a balanced approach where you devote about fifty percent of your time to the Assessment Phase and fifty percent to the Implementation Phase. From a bird's-eye view, during the Assessment Phase, you will specifically identify where operational problems or opportunities for improvement exist. You then quantify the problems or opportunities in operational terms (e.g., quality, volume, speed, etc.) as well as in financial terms, when possible (e.g., revenue, costs, operating margin, etc.). Next, you isolate and examine the causes of the problems, and then you finish this phase by benchmarking against best practices to find potential solutions.

During the Implementation Phase, you formulate the right recommendations and implement them as efficiently as possible. You then refine and monitor the implemented recommendations so that the organization can realize sustained improvements.

As you go through this process, you will find that each of the two phases is further broken down into two stages, totaling four stages. These four stages reflect the logical sequence of a performance optimization project in even greater detail. Each stage then consists of two related steps, as illustrated below:

> **PHASE I: ASSESSMENT**
> ### *Stage I: Opportunity Analysis*
> Step 1: Measure current performance
> Step 2: Establish performance targets
> ### *Stage II: Operational Review*
> Step 3: Evaluate underperforming operations
> Step 4: Benchmark best practice operations
>
> **PHASE II: IMPLEMENTATION**
> ### *Stage III: Recommendations and Implementation*
> Step 5: Recommend operational improvements
> Step 6: Implement recommendations
> ### *Stage IV: Sustainability and Refinement*
> Step 7: Monitor outcomes
> Step 8: Refine improvements

Stage I, Opportunity Analysis, consists of practical, straightforward data analytics to determine if, and to what extent, an operation can be improved. The opportunity analysis assesses the actual performance outcomes of an operation and compares it to expected or targeted outcomes (i.e., the objectives). A negative variance between actual and targeted performance indicates an opportunity for improvement. Once the performance opportunity is identified, it is converted into a financial opportunity when possible so that the costs associated with improving an operation can be compared against the financial opportunity to estimate a return on investment.

After completing the opportunity analysis, it is time to move backward, "managing in reverse," from the outputs of the operation to the operation itself. Stage II, Operational Review, outlines a sequence of eight tasks that will allow you to scrutinize the current state of an operation. These tasks help you determine where specific problems and opportunities exist and also help you identify the underlying causes of those problems. While quantitative analysis (data analysis) is necessary in this stage, qualitative analysis (non-data analysis) is also used to pinpoint specific problems and opportunities within underperforming operations. Potential solutions also emerge during this early stage.

Once Stage I and Stage II (which make up the Assessment Phase) are complete, the next task is to formulate and implement the right improvement recommendations. This is done in Stage III: Recommendations and Implementation. During this stage, recommendations are carefully evaluated, prioritized, and then implemented according to proper project management and change management principles.

The final stage, Stage IV, Sustainability and Refinement, is where you monitor and modify the implemented recommendations to ensure that the organization will realize and sustain optimal outcomes. If everything is done correctly in Stages I through III, Stage IV is the simplest stage, where changes become operationalized and persistent. Here you will continually monitor key performance indicators to make certain that performance standards are met.

As we move forward, it is important to recognize that transformation is often a much weightier call for change than performance improvement. Not all operations need drastic change. The key is to develop the right recommendations for underperforming operations so that objectives are achieved. Employing the eight steps will guarantee that the right recommendations are made, regardless of whether an operation needs to be improved or transformed.

Figure 1 outlines the eight steps of *Managing in Reverse* in a more concise format.

PHASE I. ASSESSMENT
Stage I - Opportunity Analysis
Step 1: Measure current performance
Step 2: Establish performance targets
Stage II - Operational Review
Step 3: Evaluate underperforming operations
Step 4: Benchmark best practice organizations
PHASE II. IMPLEMENTATION
Stage III - Recommendations & implementation
Step 5: Recommend operational improvements
Step 6: Implement recommendations
Stage IV - Sustainability & Refinement
Step 7: Monitor outcomes
Step 8: Refine improvements

Figure 1: **The eight steps of *Managing in Reverse***

While working through each of the sequential steps, it is important to realize that the amount of time it takes to accomplish each step can vary depending on the project, as well as the skillset and experience of those involved. Figure 2 provides an overall perspective of the relative amounts of time that are typically devoted to each of the *Managing in Reverse'* phases, stages, and steps.

	Relative Weight
PHASE I. ASSESSMENT	**50%**
Stage I - Opportunity Analysis	**15%**
Step 1: Measure current performance	10%
Step 2: Establish performance targets	5%
Stage II - Operational Review	**35%**
Step 3: Evaluate underperforming operations	25%
Step 4: Benchmark best practice organizations	10%
PHASE II. IMPLEMENTATION	**50%**
Stage III - Recommendations & implementation	**35%**
Step 5: Recommend operational improvements	10%
Step 6: Implement recommendations	25%
Stage IV - Sustainability & Refinement	**15%**
Step 7: Monitor outcomes	5%
Step 8: Refine improvements	10%

Figure 2: **Relative percentage of time dedicated to each phase, stage, and step of** *Managing in Reverse*

Figure 3 graphically illustrates the relative weights of time devoted to each of the four stages, while Figure 4 illustrates the relative weights of time devoted to each of the eight steps. These charts help you visualize the symmetry and balance of how a performance improvement project should be carried out.

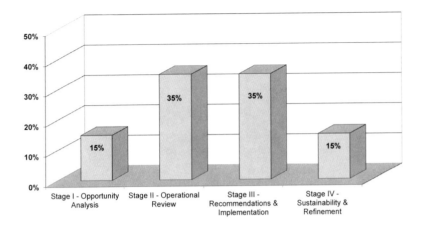

Figure 3: **Relative percentage of time dedicated to each stage**

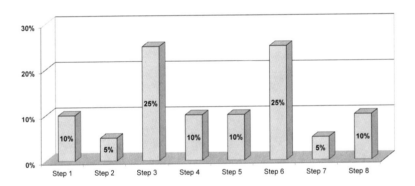

Figure 4: **Relative percentage of time dedicated to each step**

THE BASIC UNIT
OF PERFORMANCE

Before we delve into each of the eight steps of *Managing in Reverse*, it is imperative that we first understand what an operation is and how it works. Since the eight steps and their related tactics align with the anatomy and function of an operation, it is critical that an operation be defined in detail.

What Is an Operation?

In simple terms, an operation is the basic unit of performance for an organization, company, institution, or the professional work done by an individual. It is the channel or performance engine that converts inputs, through a process or series of processes, into outputs.

For instance, inputs such as iron ore, construction materials, financial information, intellectual property, or a patient can be converted through an operation into steel, a skyscraper, a prepared tax return, a patent, or a healthier person. How well an operation converts inputs into outputs in terms of cost, quality, speed, volume, and many other performance factors determines how well or how poorly it is performing. Figure 5 illustrates a simple operation with inputs and outputs.

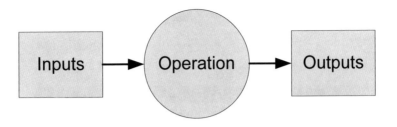

Figure 5: **Illustration of an operation**

Components of an Operation

An operation, however, encompasses much more than the physical or tactile elements that transform inputs into outputs, such as a manufacturing assembly line. An operation embodies everything—both directly and indirectly, visually and non-visually—that is required to transform inputs into outputs. These elements can be broken down into two fundamental components.

The first component of an operation represents the more tangible, nonhuman elements of the operation. These may include equipment, facilities, computer systems, vehicles, tools, location, layout, procedures, regulations, and processes that help transform inputs into outputs. Many mistakenly perceive that an operation only consists of these types of elements and consequently focus all efforts on improving them. In response, people create process flow charts, assess equipment, analyze physical space, automate processes, install new computer systems, perform time and motion studies, and so forth, to determine how to improve the tangible, non-human component of an operation.

The second component of an operation, however, and arguably more significant, represents the more intangible, human elements, consisting of leadership, organization structure, staff, culture, compensation, incentives, goals, working environment, customs, communications, and other elements that involve and affect human beings who do the work. Figure 6 depicts the two components of an operation.

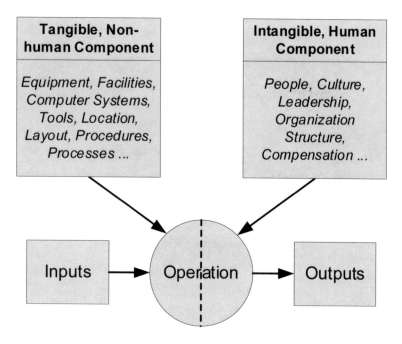

Figure 6: **The two components of an operation**

While much efficiency can be derived from improving an operation's tangible elements (e.g., computer systems, equipment, facilities, and procedures), an operation cannot be optimized without also improving its intangible components (e.g., organizational structure, leadership, staff, and culture). Therefore, optimizing an operation must balance the improvement effort between the tangible (nonhuman) and intangible (human) components.

When good leadership is intact, some operations can run quite efficiently, even when using archaic systems. On the other hand, some operations using state of the art systems barely hobble along due to poor leadership. This dynamic of leadership permeates an entire operation, affecting both the human and nonhuman components.

Operational Hierarchy

After understanding the two primary components of an operation, it is important to understand the hierarchical layers of operations within an organization. For instance, larger organizations can generally be made up of six or even more operational levels. Smaller organizations may have fewer levels. Since the actual number of levels within an organization may vary, this section describes six basic operational levels in common terms. While the names associated with each operational level may vary among organizations, the key point is that organizations are composed of an operational hierarchy, from the top down.

Organization Level: At the highest level, an operation is the entire organization. A government, university, military, steel mill, construction company, automobile manufacturing plant, financial institution, and healthcare system are examples of large operations, each converting inputs into outputs. Large organizations are made up of many underlying operations that work together to achieve the overall organization's objectives.

The outputs of some organizations become the inputs of other organizations, and this cycle can repeat itself over and over. For instance, a steel mill receives iron ore, coke, and limestone from mining companies to produce plate steel. The plate steel is then shipped to steel fabrication companies, who use it to produce steel beams. The beams are then shipped to construction companies, which use them to build bridges or buildings.

Division Level: For larger organizations, the next level of operational hierarchy is typically the division level. Some organizations may use other designations for the next level down, such as "group" or "area." But for simplicity, we will use the term "division." Divisions can be a group of subsidiary companies, geographic regions, product or service lines, brands, branches, or similar groups of departments within an organization that typically function under a common executive.

The United States government is an example of an organization with distinct objectives, where its next level down is composed of branches—the executive, legislative, and judicial bodies. These branches of government are simply sub-operations of the larger organization and could be referred to as divisions. Enormous organizations may even have divisions within divisions—or subdivisions, which add additional operational layers to the organization. The point is that each division works toward a common purpose of converting inputs into outputs. The Supreme Court of the United States, for instance, uses legal cases as their input and converts them into judgements and opinions as their output. This is a crucial role to the overall organization and operation of the government.

Business Unit Level: The third operational level is the business unit level. In a larger organization, for example, a parent company may own many stand-alone companies, or business units. As another example, a large corporation may consist of several divisions, where each is comprised of a conglomerate of similar business units such as several different grocery store chains. Each grocery store operates as a separate business unit. Much smaller organizations, like a restaurant or a law firm, are business units with fewer operational levels.

Department Level: The fourth basic operational level is the department level. Departments are the primary suboperations of a business unit. Some of the department-level operations of a hospital, for example, include radiology, critical care, anesthesia, obstetrics, neurology, urology, medical records, pathology, pharmacy, housekeeping, information technology, surgery, biomedical engineering, finance, admitting, purchasing, and a host of others. What's important is that each department works interdependently to transform inputs into outputs in order to produce the desired outcomes of the overall business unit, the hospital.

Functional Level: The fifth level of operational hierarchy is the functional level, which represents the various groups, committees, teams, and suboperations that compose a department. For instance, a hospital radiology department is often composed of several different modalities, including interventional radiology, ultrasound, fluoroscopy, magnetic resonance imaging (MRI), computed tomography (CT), nuclear medicine, positron emission tomography (PET), and x-ray. Each of these suboperations, or functional levels of the larger department, is working to convert inputs, such as imaging film, contrast media, and patients, into outputs—accurate diagnostics. Each functional area helps the overall department fulfill its critical role within the organization.

Work Task Level: The sixth level of operational hierarchy is the work task level, where functional areas are further broken down into isolated work tasks. In a construction company, this is where shingles are nailed to the roof, sheetrock is hung, paint is sprayed on the walls, plumbing is installed, and carpet is laid.

Figure 7 provides an example of the six primary levels of operations within an organization.

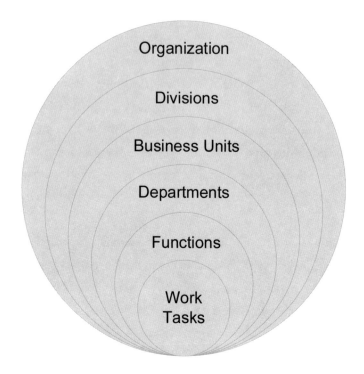

Figure 7: **Example of different levels of operations within an organization**

Complex Operations and the Human Body Analogy

The human body provides an excellent analogy for the various levels of operational hierarchy in an organization. At the highest level, the body is an operation, akin to an overall organization that converts inputs into outputs. For example, inputs such as food, knowledge, and sensory information are converted into outputs such as energy and action, thoughts and ideas, emotion and responses.

At the next level, the body consists of ten physiological systems, which include the cardiovascular, digestive, endocrine, immune, muscular, nervous, renal, reproductive, respiratory, and skeletal systems. These systems are analogous to the divisions of an organization that convert inputs into outputs. For instance, the cardiovascular system has several vital functions, such as transporting blood throughout the body and bringing oxygen and nutrients to the cells while removing metabolic waste.

Broken down further, physiological systems are composed of many suboperations, such as the heart, lung, brain, liver, kidneys, and other vital organs. These are analogous to business units within larger organizations. Each organ can be broken down further into suboperations, akin to departments within the operational hierarchy, such as the four chambers of the heart or the four lobes of the brain. The chambers of the heart and lobes of the brain consist of further suboperations that work together to generate critical outputs for that particular organ. The heart, for example, is comprised of two upper chambers called atria and two lower chambers called ventricles, all of which work together to pump blood through the lungs and body. The parietal lobe of the brain is made of left and right regions that process sensory information.

Further operational breakdowns in the vital organs and systems of the body can occur down to functional levels and then to the most isolated work tasks performed by the smallest cell. But regardless of the number and levels of operations and suboperations, whether found within the human body or within an organization, each operation converts inputs to outputs in a sequential or concurrent manner that ultimately combines and culminates into producing outputs, as depicted in Figures 8 and 9.

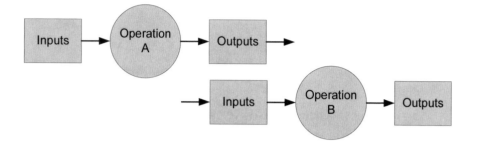

Figure 8: **Sequential operations A and B (where the outputs of A become the inputs of B)**

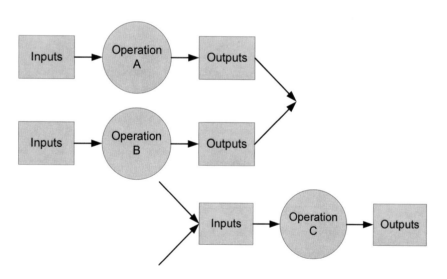

Figure 9: **Concurrent operations A and B (where the outputs of A and B become the inputs of C)**

Some organizations seem so vast and complex that, like the human body, it is a management miracle that the intended outcomes are ever realized. Speaking of hospitals, Peter Drucker had said, "Even small healthcare institutions are complex, barely manageable places … Large healthcare institutions, may be the most complex organizations in human history" (Peter Drucker, *Post-Capitalist Society*. New York, Harper and Row, 1993).

Like organizations, professional individuals also function within a series of operations, often composed of suboperations and sub-suboperations. Take, for instance, a surgeon, a house painter, a bricklayer, a certified public accountant, a professional athlete, or a chef. Each professional performs sequential or concurrent operations and work tasks to reach their desired outcomes. A chef may have rolls baking in the oven, ribs cooking on the grill, shrimp cocktail chilling in the refrigerator, chocolate mousse cooling, and asparagus soup simmering—all while he or she is slicing tomatoes for a salad. Each task is a separate operation, with inputs and outputs, within an overall operation that eventually must combine into a five-course meal.

Yet, no matter how vast and complex an operation may seem, when broken down into operational hierarchical levels—from the organization as a whole to the smallest work task—organizations become quite comprehensible and even manageable. Puzzle pieces start to fit together, and the complex becomes simple. And regardless of which operational level in the organizational hierarchy needs to be improved—whether the organization as a whole, a suboperation, or a specific work task—the approach and methodology to improve an operation are the same.

Deliverables Determine Success

Now that we have discussed the anatomy of an operation in some detail, we need to turn our attention to the function of an operation—not how it functions but rather its objective, or the purpose it serves. We now know that an operation is a conversion process where inputs are converted into outputs. In the end, the success of an operation boils down to the cost, quality, speed, quantity, and other factors associated with the outputs, outcomes, or deliverables of the operation.

In fact, organizations, companies, institutions, and professional individuals succeed or fail, live or die, based on their outcomes—what they deliver. This is because deliverables—the products and services produced and offered by an organization or professional individual—represent the quality, price, speed of delivery, utility, service, and overall experience of the product or service that customers purchase.

Because typical consumers try to optimize their purchasing power by buying products and services that provide the best value, organizations and professionals who cannot deliver optimal outcomes risk being displaced by someone who can. Until someone can deliver, consumers typically won't purchase a poor product or service. On the other hand, if someone can deliver a great product or service, new business and repeat business soar.

To further illustrate this point, in 1985, the Utah Jazz of the National Basketball Association recruited a six-foot-nine-inch tall junior power forward from Louisiana Tech named Karl Malone. During his first year with the Jazz, Malone was astounding and was named to the 1985–86 NBA All-Rookie Team. Over the next eighteen years, this superstar became widely known as one of the greatest power forwards of all time. Malone was tough. He played with poise and finesse. Because of his athleticism, skill, and confidence, he consistently delivered points, rebounds, and free throws—things that won games. In fact, Malone was nicknamed "The Mailman" because "he always delivered." Fans came to watch the two-time NBA MVP and two-time Olympic gold medalist receive assists from his counterpart, point guard John Stockton (an NBA leader in assists and steals). Malone muscled his way to the basket, slammed the ball through the hoop, or took a last-second fade-away jumper while drawing a defensive foul. It was spectacular. And "The Mailman" delivered game after game, year after year.

Malone was so relentless in his delivery that in 1996, he was named one of the fifty greatest players in NBA history, as was his teammate, John Stockton. Malone was also selected to the All-NBA First Team eleven times and fourteen times as an NBA All-Star. At the end of his career, The Mailman was second in total points ever scored (only behind Kareem Abdul-Jabbar). He was also an all-time leader in defensive rebounds and had made the most free throws in NBA history.

Since The Mailman always delivered a great product, he was highly successful, as was the Utah Jazz basketball organization at that time. Spectators purchased tickets to watch Stockton assist Malone, who delivered the points. The two of them helped take the Utah Jazz to two NBA finals with the Chicago Bulls, in 1997 and 1998. Consumer ticket purchases, satisfaction, and entertainment levels were at an all-time high. However, once Stockton and Malone moved on or retired, the team's success and number of wins declined, and seemingly, so did customer satisfaction. It was now time for the Jazz to rebuild its operation to recreate the deliverables and outcomes fans had previously enjoyed.

Deliverables Reflect the Quality of the Operation

Deliverables are the end result. As the final outcome of an operation or series of operations, deliverables are the measuring stick of an operation's performance. Take, for instance, "His Airness," Michael Jordan. Some still argue that he was the greatest basketball player of all time and the one player whom John Stockton and Karl Malone from the Utah Jazz could not overcome in both the 1997 and 1998 NBA finals games (Utah Jazz versus Chicago Bulls). What were the deliverables of "His Airness?" To name a few, he was NBA rookie of the year in 1985, five-time NBA MVP, ten-time NBA first team selection, member of six NBA national championship teams, two-time Olympic gold medalist, and when entering his 2002–03 season, he ranked first in NBA history in scoring with an average of thirty-one points per game. These outcomes manifested that Jordan's on-the-court operation was simply the best. The NBA is known for saying: "By acclamation, Michael Jordan is the greatest basketball player of all time. Although a summary of his basketball career and influence on the game inevitably fails to do it justice, as a phenomenal athlete with a unique combination of fundamental soundness, grace, speed, power, artistry, improvisational ability, and an unquenchable competitive desire, Jordan single-handedly redefined the NBA superstar."

Watching Michael Jordan play basketball—or watching the operation that produced the points—was as remarkable an experience for fans as were his end-of-game results. In fact, because his deliverables were so unparalleled, his on-the-court operation literally became a product in and of itself. Said another way, Jordan's on-the-court operation was so thrilling to watch that it became a quasi-deliverable itself. His remarkable athleticism attracted millions of spectators.

Yet if Jordan hadn't been able to deliver points, no one would have come to watch him hang in the air until he decided to come down. As Magic Johnson said, "Once Michael gets up there, he says, 'Well, maybe I'll just hang up here in the air for a while, just sit back.' Then all of a sudden, he says, 'Well, maybe I'll do a 360. No, I changed my mind. I'll go up on the other side.' He's just incredible." But remarkable athleticism doesn't matter much if it is not followed by the desired outcome—a ball through the hoop—which Jordan could convert with stellar regularity.

Simply put, outstanding deliverables—such as products and services—reflect outstanding operations, while poor deliverables reflect poor operations. The reverse is highly unlikely to occur, where poor operations produce outstanding deliverables. Neither do outstanding operations produce poor deliverables.

For many, observing an operation that produces great deliverables can be as satisfying as the outcome itself, as in watching Michael Jordan play basketball. This is why resident physicians learn by observing experienced surgeons perform surgical operations that result in successful patient outcomes; why business people study great automobile manufacturing processes that produce the best cars; and why consumers visit beverage, donut, and chocolate factories that produce delicious products. The operations themselves are exciting, impressive, and instructive to observe.

Yet if the end products and services of these thrilling-to-watch operations didn't produce superb outcomes, few people would ever observe and learn from these operations, no matter how spectacular. In fact, many companies actually build businesses based upon their unique and impressive operations and flirt with them in front of customers as their primary product. However, if these businesses cannot deliver a great outcome, they are on shaky ground and are destined to failure.

The quality of the end-product or service is always more important than the operation that produced them, no matter how impressive the operation is to watch. After first retiring from professional basketball, Michael Jordan played one year of minor league baseball, where he proved to be a less-than-thrilling player to watch. Why? Because in 1994, his .202 batting average wasn't a spectacular outcome.

Deliverables Are the Starting Point

The surest and easiest way to tell if an operation is extraordinary or if it needs improvement is to first examine its deliverables and then move backwards, "managing in reverse," from there to the operation. The world of sports has mastered this concept. Outcome statistics are kept on every level of an operation—including every season, every team, every game, every component of every game, and from every coach on down to every player.

These statistics are monitored because they reveal whether an overall operation or its suboperations need improvement and, if so, in what specific areas. For instance, in college football, overall statistics are tracked based on each team's win-loss records, national rankings, and bowl game championships. At the next level down, suboperations are measured. For instance, total points scored, total rushing yards, and total passing yards are tracked for the offensive squad. For the defensive squad, points allowed, number of sacks, number of interceptions, and other metrics are tracked. At the next level down, statistics are tracked for each player, such as the average yards per carry for a running back.

Team owners and coaches then review the outcome statistics and move backwards, "managing in reverse," to adjust the various levels of operations. For instance, a consistently poor win-loss record usually results in a new head coach. Poor offensive yards per game results in new plays, modified offensive line-ups, and more intense training and practices. Low average yards per carry can result in a change of running backs.

In fact, consumers imitate these exercises, although they may do so subconsciously. For instance, consumers also use deliverables as their gauge to evaluate or judge a company that produces the products and services they purchase. Bad products and services equate to a bad company; good products and services equate to a good company.

Consumers often know very little about the operation that produces the products and services they buy. Consumers typically just want the best product and service for their money. The instant consumers perceive products and services are poor or trending downward in terms of quality, utility, customer service, price, and so forth, they find replacement products—just as coaches and sports team owners make coaching and player changes.

However, as intuitive as this concept is—using deliverables as the gauge to determine whether operational problems exist and need improvement—countless leaders, managers, committees, and professionals bypass this step and don't collect all the necessary outcomes data before trying to fix an operation. It is like trying to improve Michael Jordan's game without gathering the outcomes statistics on his points, rebounds, steals, and assists to specify the exact areas where improvements can be made.

Deliverables Reflect or Define Business Objectives

Finally, it is essential to understand that deliverables reveal much more than whether an operation is thriving or failing. Deliverables also reflect—perhaps even define—the strategy, mission, vision, goals, and values of an organization.

If deliverables reflect pre-established business objectives of an organization—including a well-formulated business strategic plan, documented mission and vision statements, and goals that hang on the walls of the organization—then the operations are most likely very efficient and productive. This is because the operations are intentionally aligned with and driven by the organization's business objectives.

For example, the mission statement of the world-renowned Mayo Clinic is "to inspire hope and contribute to health and well-being by providing *the best care* to every patient through integrated clinical practice, education, and research." It is worthy to note that Mayo Clinic's deliverables are consistent with its pre-established mission. The Mayo Clinic carries a tradition of excellence and is consistently ranked among the top hospitals in the nation by *U.S. News & World Report.* In fact, not only does this hospital system usually rank among the very top hospitals in the nation, but as expected, many of its service lines, including cardiology and heart surgery; diabetes and endocrinology; ear, nose, and throat; gastroenterology and GI surgery; geriatrics; gynecology; nephrology; neurology and neurosurgery; ophthalmology; orthopedics; and psychiatry, also receive top national rankings. This illustrates that its health system's suboperational levels are aligned to the mission of the overall institution. What the Mayo Clinic espouses to do, and what it actually delivers, are consistent with one another.

On the other hand, if the deliverables of an organization communicate something other than its business objectives (i.e., its strategy, mission, vision, goals, and values), then the organization's operations are misaligned and not functioning toward a common goal. In such cases, by default, the deliverables of the organization define the business objectives of the organization, or they signify a lack of them. Consequently, these organizations reveal that their administrative team has relinquished the control and governance of their operations into the hands of their directors and managers, who are not working in unison toward a common goal.

When this occurs, competing strategies emerge and contend with one another, causing poor outcomes. Costs also spiral out of control as the organization becomes inefficient and fragmented. Differing market niches and consumer demographic populations are served, quality fluctuates, the amount of time to produce a product or deliver a service is elongated, and the organization loses its competitive foothold.

This scenario is a case of operations by inertia, wherein the various directors and managers have taken over the guidance of an organization in an ineffective, noncollaborative manner. Like a basketball team without a coach or a military unit without a commander, it's every man for himself because there is no overall plan or authority to construct and direct the plan. Such organizations are heading for disaster—or an expensive consulting turnaround engagement.

To illustrate, I once consulted a retail department store chain. As I interviewed a host of people from administration, finance, store management, marketing, human resources, purchasing, shipping and receiving, product stocking, and floor sales, not one person—even from administration, could explain the strategic plan, mission, vision, goals, or values of the organization. No one could identify the chain's target market, its competitors, the demographics of its consumer population, or even whether the organization was a high-end, high-quality or low-end, low-priced department store.

I still recall the purchasing manager telling me that he purchased both high-end, name-brand clothing items as well as inexpensive men's white dress shirts that he knew he could "blow out" during a big sale. Nobody could articulate the organization's competitive advantage, its core competencies, or its strategic market position. As a result, the various suboperations of the company—from marketing and sales to procurement and administration—were in disarray. Not long afterwards, the organization was bought out by another department store chain.

Emphatically, the operations of an organization must be directed by and aligned with the business objectives of the overall organization. In one medical center where I consulted, they had a particular patient care department that had been losing millions for several years. I discovered that the department was not contributing to the business objectives of the health system. The health system's threefold mission was excellence in teaching, research, and patient care. Its financial goals were to provide patient care services while remaining financially viable. However, in this department, no student teaching or research was taking place. And while the department was providing good, quality patient care, it was doing so at heavy financial losses. Therefore, we closed the department rather than try to fix it because it was misaligned and not contributing to the overall business objectives of the institution.

Operations that are not directed by and aligned with the organization's business objectives must be significantly altered or eliminated. In some cases, however, an organization may have obsolete business objectives that require updating. Figure 10 illustrates the concept of how an operation must be aligned with current business objectives of the organization rather than the other way around, where the various operations actually direct the organization.

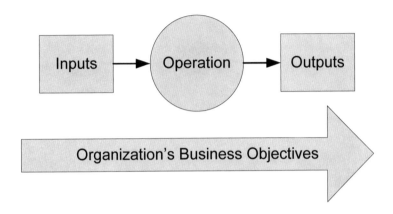

Figure 10: **Alignment of an operation to an organization's business objectives**

CHAPTER SUMMARY: Key Points

1. An operation is the basic unit of performance of an organization, company, institution, or professional individual and is what converts inputs into outputs, outcomes, or deliverables.

2. Two components make up an operation. The tangible, nonhuman component comprises equipment, facilities, computer systems, vehicles, tools, location, layout, procedures, and regulations. The intangible, human component includes leadership, organization structure, staff, culture, compensation, incentives, goals, working environment, customs, communications, and other factors involving or affecting human beings. To optimize the performance and outcomes of an operation, there must be a balanced focus on improving each component.

3. Organizations are composed of an operational hierarchy from the top down. Large organizations, for instance, can be made up of at least six primary operational levels: the overall organization, divisions, business units, departments, functions, and work tasks. Small organizations may have fewer levels.

4. Operations and suboperations work sequentially or concurrently to transform inputs into outputs.

5. Larger organizations consist of a complex series of operations and suboperations analogous to the structure of the human body. However, when broken down according

to their operational hierarchy, a complex organization becomes quite comprehensible and manageable.

6. The outputs, outcomes, or deliverables of an operation determine the success or failure of an organization, company, institution, or professional individual.

7. Deliverables reflect the quality of an operation. Superior deliverables reflect superior operations, while poor deliverables reflect poor operations.

8. Optimizing performance starts with assessing deliverables. The next step is to move backwards, "managing in reverse," to the operation, and then to the inputs.

9. Deliverables either reflect or they define an organization's objectives (i.e., its strategy, mission, vision, goals, and values).

10. Operations must be aligned with current business objectives. Incongruous operations must be significantly altered or eliminated, or the business objectives must be updated and modified.

STEP 1

Measure Current Performance

PHASE I. ASSESSMENT
Stage I - Opportunity Analysis
Step 1: Measure current performance
Step 2: Establish performance targets
Stage II - Operational Review
Step 3: Evaluate underperforming operations
Step 4: Benchmark best practice organizations
PHASE II. IMPLEMENTATION
Stage III - Recommendations & implementation
Step 5: Recommend operational improvements
Step 6: Implement recommendations
Stage IV - Sustainability & Refinement
Step 7: Monitor outcomes
Step 8: Refine improvements

As we dive into the eight steps to optimizing performance, let's imagine that you were a consultant doing the work rather than a leader overseeing the work. This ground-level perspective will give you greater insight into the important details of how each step is carried out and what to look for. So, let's roll up our sleeves and get into the weeds just a bit.

The first step is to measure the current performance of an operation by examining its outputs, outcomes, or deliverables. You should devote approximately ten percent of a performance improvement project to this step. Its companion step, Step 2, will help you establish performance targets and calculate improvement opportunities (discussed in the next chapter). Combined, these two steps constitute Stage 1, Opportunity Analysis, and provide a data-driven approach to help you identify underperforming operations and sub-operations that need improvement or even transformation.

As discussed in the previous chapter, deliverables are the starting point for optimizing improvement and operational excellence because they indicate how well an operation is performing and whether it needs improvement. Unfortunately, however, many organizations try to fix operations they believe need improvement based on perceptions and anecdotes instead of consulting the data. While this approach sometimes works, it is usually hit or miss because it provides no road map for identifying which operations and suboperations need improvement based upon empirical evidence.

Transforming an operation without the data to support the need for improvement can be highly risky—like shooting blindfolded. This approach can result in the loss of both financial and human capital. Not only do misfires rarely hit the bull's-eye, they often backfire, causing significant rework, frustration, and irreparable damage.

For instance, when an improvement project is unsuccessful—such as trying to transform an operation that needs little or no improving or attempting to improve an operation where there is no projected return on investment—you can spend significant resources on new systems and equipment that don't yield offsetting gains. At greater risk, however, are the costs of human capital, such as an administrative team that loses trust and credibility, disgruntled high-performing employees who leave the organization, staff who lose confidence in future improvement initiatives, and a once happy and productive working culture breaking down.

The main objective of the opportunity analysis is to clearly identify what specific operations and sub-operations need to be improved and to what extent. Organizations that get into the never-ending debate of whether they should centralize or decentralize, outsource or insource, separate or combine work functions, simply haven't arrived at any conclusive answers and shouldn't proceed until they have. Performance improvement and operational transformation should not be based on a conjecture or gamble, but on a decision that is clearly the right move based on data.

Key Performance Indicators

Step 1 in the assessment phase is also crucial because it lays the foundation for the other seven steps. Step 1 involves referencing key performance indicators (KPIs), or metrics, that track the current and critical outcomes of the operation being scrutinized. If critical KPIs are not set up and easily accessible, then this is the step where they should be created or revamped. While this can add more time to completing this step, it is crucial.

In fact, it is so crucial because all the remaining steps build upon and correlate to the KPIs. Though this step is straightforward and the principles surrounding it are self-evident, I am constantly surprised at how many people skip over it and go right to an operation and try to fix it. When improvement projects begin this way, followed by quickly formulating and implementing recommendations without first reviewing the outcomes that show where the problems occur, that project is nearly always destined to fail.

To start, I have found that the best format for setting up and monitoring KPIs is to track them in a concise, high-level format known as a dashboard, similar to the dashboard of an airplane. A dashboard provides critical traveling information such as speed, altitude, fuel, and distance. Using this type of format, KPIs show the basic vital signs of an operation and tell management at a glance how well it is performing.

Operational KPIs track crucial outcomes that are associated with key financial statements (such as revenue, costs, and net income), productivity, volume, quality, speed, customer feedback, employee satisfaction, and so forth. Additional KPIs can be developed and customized as needed.

Components of KPI Dashboards

To determine what essential outcomes should be measured and how these data should be reported on your KPI dashboard, apply the following eight components:

1. KPI dashboards must be succinct and only track the outcomes of an operation that correspond to its primary purposes and objectives. Asking questions such as, "What is the purpose or objective of this operation?" Or, "What is this operation's reason for being?" will help determine the critical outcomes you need to track. Unfortunately, some operations do not seem to have a clearly defined purpose or objective, which causes uncertainty about why they exist or what performance metrics to track. In these cases, the purpose of the operation must be defined before the critical outcomes can be determined and measured. Furthermore, KPIs that are not germane to the purposes and objectives of the operation should not be tracked because they are irrelevant. Although this seems commonsense, it is nonetheless surprising how many managers track irrelevant data. In addition, even if an operation is tracking the right data, frequently the data is either excessive or insufficient.

While tracking insufficient data certainly won't lead an operation down the targeted path to optimal performance, neither will gathering, analyzing, and reporting excessive data. Over-reporting requires time and resources. In addition, over-reporting can create ambiguity, just as insufficient data creates uncertainty.

As a new vice president for a large health system, I was furnished with a huge stack of reports from each of my directors, representing their month-end financial, productivity, and labor reports. Each stack of reports was so thick and the data formatted in such a variety of charts and graphs that I didn't have time to summarize it and make sense of it. As a result, the data was not helpful to me in assessing the performance of the operations for which I was responsible.

My first task, therefore, was to recreate a set of new KPI dashboards for each director. These new KPIs would only measure critical indicators as simply as possible. I then consolidated and summarized each of the directors' dashboards onto a higher-level dashboard that went to my boss and to the board of directors. For the first time, they could see at a glance how my area was performing. The new, concise dashboards were meaningful and efficient, and they quickly indicated the pulse of the operations I oversaw. As a byproduct, the number of analysts and their associated costs required to generate the new reports were reduced.

2. KPIs must be aligned with and contribute to the business objectives (i.e., the strategy, mission, vision, goals, and values) of the

overall organization. Critical performance outcomes that must be measured are also those that contribute to and align with the business objectives of the overall organization. This is because the business objectives are the stimuli that created the operations in the first place and are responsible for their existence. Therefore, as mentioned in the preceding chapter, operations and suboperations whose outcomes do not align with and contribute to fulfilling the business objectives of the overall organization must be modified or eliminated. Conversely, if operational outcomes are on track but misaligned with the organization's business objectives, it may very well be that the business objectives are old and need updating.

To ensure that operations align with business objectives, KPIs should be developed to track only those outcomes that are relevant to the overall organization. Leaders should then hold staff accountable to those aligned KPIs so that all operations are focused on accomplishing the objectives of the broader organization. When all operations within an organization are thus aligned, the whole organization becomes more efficient, productive, and streamlined as it functions toward common goals. In fact, employees are happier because they are working toward common objectives and recognize how their work is meaningful and contributes to the big picture.

While I was working in senior management for a large organization, the executive team had established business goals for the entire institution. After communicating these goals to the rest of the management, administration asked that every director and manager align their goals with those of the institution. In essence, the greater goals of the organization were divided among the departments, and each department was held accountable for accomplishing its part. Some goals were financially related, such as staying within budget; others dealt with reaching specified volume goals; still others dealt with customer satisfaction, employee turn-over, and quality goals. The only factor that departments were evaluated on that year was accomplishing their part of the organization's overall goals. At the end of the year, the organization's business objectives were reached, and the administration had elevated its overall performance.

3. KPIs should be tracked at the proper time intervals. Tracking KPIs daily may be more useful than weekly; weekly tracking may be more useful than monthly; and monthly tracking may be more useful than quarterly. By accelerating the time intervals of KPI reports, managers can increase their response time to problems. In addition, employees will often improve their performance not only when it is tracked but when it is tracked more frequently.

On the other hand, it may be more practical to track some KPIs less frequently. Over-tracking can cause employees to feel micromanaged, not trusted, and even demoralized because they feel no latitude or freedom in their work. In addition, over-reporting consumes resources and is a non-value-added exercise.

While the principle of proper and timely reporting is quite intuitive, as a consultant, I have often had to adjust the time intervals in which KPIs were tracked and reported in both directions—more or less frequently, according to the needs of the organization.

4. KPIs must be accurate. Regardless of whether KPI dashboards are already in place or need to be created to report the outcomes of an operation, the data they report must be accurate. You cannot afford to trust data that has not been verified when identifying underperforming operations. All too often, I have found inaccurate and unreliable KPIs.

While directing a massive supply chain improvement project at a renowned hospital system, we found that the data in the materials management information system was not accurate. Different nomenclature was used in naming the various supply items. In addition, product pricing was out of date, manufacturing item numbers were not maintained, and obsolete items still existed in the system as products that could be purchased. Using the data for analysis was virtually impossible because approximately half the data was wrong or missing. To clean up the data, we had to hire a firm to pull the entire database, scrub it, and then upload the clean information back into the system—an expensive process.

In another case, when I was facilitating an operational improvement project in a particular hospital's emergency department, I found that its most recent annual operating statement showed that the department had generated millions of dollars for the bottom line. However, after going through the details that made up the operating statement, we found that revenue was highly overstated. After painstakingly recalculating the correct net revenue for the department, we found that it was actually losing money. Imagine how differently the department director would have managed her area if she had known she was operating in the red.

5. Dashboards should contain historical data to reflect trends and improvement. Four common techniques are frequently used to show performance trends. You can use one or all of these on your dashboards as necessary.

- The first technique is to compare current performance to a series of the most recent historical data. For instance, you could compare current productivity to three prior weeks of productivity data. Or you could compare current costs to the last three months of cost data. Recent historical figures can be listed in side-by-side columns, such as representing the different months of a year, or on simple bar charts or line graphs where trend lines can easily depict increasing or decreasing performance. Unfavorable trends indicate the need for immediate corrective action before problems become acute.

- Second, historical data can be averaged and then compared against current performance to expose trends. For instance, if a large organization is tracking its facility and engineering costs, it might want to compare its current month's costs to an average of the last three months' costs. This way, irregular monthly spikes or decreases are averaged over a quarter. This normalization of historical data allows the current month's costs to be compared against a truer representation of past costs. Three-month, or quarterly averages, are rolled forward with each new month.

- Third, dashboards can include year-to-date figures, which are the performance data for the current year that lead up to the present time. For instance, if the beginning of a fiscal year is July 1, KPI dashboards would show the performance data from July 1 to the present time. Year-to-date figures can then be averaged, totaled, trended, and projected out to see if year-end goals will be met. Year-to-date figures and trending are especially important for tracking financial information such as revenue, costs, operating margin, and other data connected to year-end goals.

- Fourth, dashboards can also compare current performance to the performance of the same time period in the previous year, representing year-over-year data. For instance, a current month's revenue could be compared against the revenue for the same month of the previous year. A percentage change could then be calculated to reflect the increase or decrease in revenue.

The purpose of comparing current performance to historical performance is to understand the trajectory of the operation's performance. This comparison, also called trending, helps determine if an operation is heading in the right direction. Trending can also help determine if a current measurement indicating poor performance is only temporary, such as a sudden change in the stock market, or if more serious issues are at hand.

Accurate trending enables you to make future projections. These projections, in turn, help you make the right improvements in a timely manner so that an operation can reach its targets. For instance, the financial hemorrhaging of an organization operating in the red may compel immediate, invasive action, whereas a slow bleed may allow more time to implement ideal, permanent solutions. Furthermore, if performance is trending in a slightly positive direction, less invasive changes may be necessary to optimize performance.

While relatively smaller amounts of historical data are usually sufficient to assess and trend performance on a KPI dashboard, at times it may be necessary to analyze more data to really understand current performance. In these one-off cases, additional historical data doesn't necessarily need to be added to the dashboard but can be analyzed separately. Going back six months is usually the minimum amount of data required to trend and assess performance, while a full year is more effective to account for seasonality. However, to gain a truly accurate historical perspective, it is generally good to review data over a three-year period. Going back further than three years is usually unnecessary and irrelevant.

6. Dashboards should contain baselines to track improvement. When performance improvement projects are underway, dashboards should contain baselines against which future performance can be tracked. Baselines are the unchanging statistics or metrics that mark how an operation is performing, and they should be in place before you begin a performance improvement project. By taking the difference between the baseline and each successive performance period, you can quantify the progress or regress of operational outcomes.

7. KPIs should include volume drivers. Current and historical financial data, such as costs, revenue, and net income, should be divided by a "volume driver" to analyze performance more accurately and from a different perspective. For instance, because of seasonality or shifts in consumer demand, operations can experience fluctuations in their month-to-month revenues and expenses. To help level out month-to-month trends, financial data should be divided by a volume driver.

For example, suppose that for three years a company's annual revenue was $500 million, $550 million, and $600 million, respectively. On the surface, these numbers show an annual growth rate of about ten percent a year. But what if the number of customers remained flat at 10,000 a year? Dividing the annual revenue by the number of customers shows that the revenue per customer increased from $50,000 in the first year ($500 million / 10,000 customers), to $55,000 in the second year ($550 million / 10,000 customers), and to

$60,000 ($600,000 million / 10,000 customers) in the third year. If the customer base didn't grow, then revenue came from price increases, up-sells, or something else. This paints a different picture than merely stating that revenue increased year over year.

To further illustrate, suppose that the same company's expenses stayed at $400 million over three years, but the customer base dropped from 10,000 in year one to 9,000 in year two and to 8,000 in year three. In this case, the expense per customer would have increased from $40,000 ($400 million / 10,000 customers) in year one to $44,444 ($400 million / 9,000 customers) in year two, and to $50,000 ($400 million / 8,000 customers) in year three. Although overall costs did not increase, which may look good on the surface, the cost per customer increased. The question is why? The next step would be to examine each expense line item in the operating statement and divide each of these numbers by the number of customers to identify where the operating costs increased the most. Was it in labor or in non-labor costs? Volume drivers can be used in a variety of ways to identify operational issues and problems.

8. KPIs must include performance targets. While we will cover performance targets in the next chapter, it is important to briefly mention that performance targets must be included on KPI dashboards because they provide the expected performance goals of an operation. Therefore, they must be consistently present on dashboards to make everyone aware of the performance expectations. Any negative variance between current and targeted performance reveals a performance gap that must be closed. Performance targets placed on dashboards can be a strong motivating factor to help influence staff in achieving goals. They are also an essential management tool for holding staff accountable for expected deliverables.

Expediency of KPIs

Once KPI dashboards have been developed, it is important to understand their value and use. KPI dashboards provide five key purposes that are explained as follows:

1. KPI dashboards are used to conduct operational assessments. Fundamentally, KPIs are used to assess the current performance of an operation. However, if there are no targets to compare current performance against, it is nearly impossible to determine whether the performance is good or bad. The difference between the current and targeted performance indicates how well an operation is performing and whether there is an opportunity for improvement. The next chapter, Step 2, discusses this in detail.

2. KPI dashboards are management tools. Because KPI dashboards continually monitor the outcomes of an operation, they alert managers to problems in a timely manner. Managers functioning without the benefit of dashboards may never know if there is a problem until it becomes acute and quite costly to repair. For instance, if product quality problems emerge and are not caught, bad product may end up on the market. Enormous recalls may then be required, resulting in significant financial costs, customer losses, and a damaged reputation.

To optimize the use of KPI dashboards as a management tool, they should be set up at each of the levels of operational hierarchy within an organization. The six basic operational levels, discussed previously, reflect the standard management levels common in most large organizations. These levels may vary based on the size of the organization. In general business terms, the associated management levels typically include the CEO, presidents, vice presidents, directors, managers, and supervisors. (For simplicity, I will include the chiefs at the CEO level.) Figure 11 depicts the basic management titles for each of the six hierarchical operational levels.

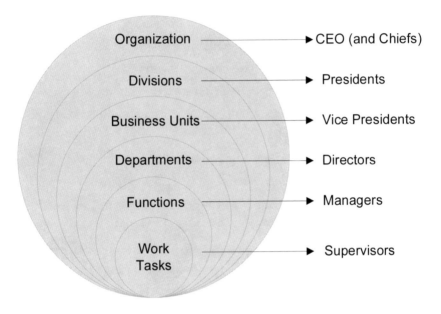

Figure 11: **KPI dashboards should correspond to the management levels within an operational hierarchy.**

When KPIs signify a problem at a particular operational level, the appropriate level of management can promptly respond. When additional information is needed to pinpoint the problem, management can review the KPI dashboards at the next level down. For instance, if a month-end operating statement shows that an organization's overall labor costs were high (compared to target), then the divisional, business unit, and department-level operating statements can be successively reviewed to identify what specific areas are causing the higher costs. Some organizations are so private that they do not allow their mid-level managers to see the financial operating statements for the areas they lead. This can pose limitations on how effectively managers can run their areas.

Surprisingly, however, when KPIs indicate that an operation is running well, some organizations still try to fix it. I recall working for a highly profitable, well-managed organization that tried to overhaul an already effectively performing operation. The "invasive surgery" it performed on the operation had appeared to be more damaging than helpful, as employee morale and a once happy and productive working culture was destroyed.

If an operation is highly efficient and operating at peak performance, like Michael Jordan on the basketball court, only potentially minor gains remain. Often, these small gains are not worth the resources and investment required to achieve them, especially when other areas of higher priority need improvement. Because the purpose of an assessment is to identify operations that clearly must be improved, organizations should devote their resources to fixing operations that actually need improvement rather than those that don't.

I remember consulting a hospital that just wanted to "fix something." During the assessment phase of the consulting engagement, my team and I found that most of the operations were performing very well. Well-set objectives were being achieved. However, hospital administration was anxious and told us during a meeting, "We just want to fix something!" I was surprised by that remark.

While some remaining improvement gains may be made on already well-performing operations, transformation is certainly unnecessary. In these cases, it is wise to follow the axiom, "*If it ain't broke, don't fix it*," because you will probably make it worse.

3. KPI dashboards make future, one-time operational assessments unnecessary. Because dashboards are ongoing monitoring devices, conducting exhaustive operational assessments is typically unnecessary. I recall hearing the CEO of a large health system explain that every five years he hires a consulting firm to assess the performance of his entire organization. However, if the right KPIs were set up to track relevant outcomes on a monthly and weekly basis, these five-year assessments and most other "one-off" analyses would be largely unnecessary. The dashboards would continually monitor the performance of the operation, thus enabling a constant performance review.

4. KPI dashboards increase productivity. When KPI dashboards are established to measure the critical outcomes of an operation for the first time, it is not uncommon for productivity to suddenly increase. The reason for this sudden increase is that when performance is unexpectedly in the spotlight, employees begin to feel increased purpose, pressure, and accountability. However, this fairly immediate surge in performance is commonly referred to as the "Hawthorne Effect." While there may be an initial surge in performance, it is commonly followed by a decline, which then levels off.

One way to sustain higher levels of performance is to produce KPI dashboards that show individual performance. When groups of employees, who are performing the same function, see how their individual performance compares to that of their peers, they tend to feel a heightened sense of personal value, ownership, and accountability. In fact, some managers like to place KPI dashboards, which show individual performance, on computer monitors mounted on the walls of visible work areas.

Dashboards that only show how the overall company, department, or team is performing may tend to improve performance, but only to a certain degree. Some leaders get overly caught up in the team approach at the expense of not driving individual performance and accountability enough. But since a team's overall performance is no better than the performance of each of the individuals who comprise it, a leader must sustain reasonable pressure on each individual.

5. KPI dashboards produce leaner operations. People at all six levels of an organizational hierarchy, from the CEO down to the frontline worker, typically perform according to what is being measured, not to mention what is being rewarded. This is because what is measured denotes what is most important. When goals are also shown on dashboards, staff are even more motivated to accomplish them because of the potential for reward and personal satisfaction.

As staff are driven and focused on accomplishing measurable goals, they become more efficient and are less likely to engage in work that does not contribute to achieving important targets. The overall result is that operations become leaner and more efficient as each employee directs their energy toward more effectively performing the right work in the most proficient way. Thus, the measurement of individual performance has a direct bearing on overall operational efficiency. It's bewildering when I see organizations distribute bonuses that have no direct bearing on reaching the most critical goals or operational outcomes.

Relative Amount of Work for Step 1 and Each Step

This is a good time to emphasize that although Step 1 is a critical and integral part of a successful operations improvement project, you would be wise not to devote excessive amounts of time and resources to this step or to any of the other eight performance improvement steps. For instance, once you have identified underperforming operations and calculated the associated financial opportunities, it is time to implement the steps that lead to actual gains. In my experience, far too much time and resources can be spent overanalyzing data rather than actually implementing improvements. Therefore, while each step must be completed, it must be executed efficiently. Figure 12 again outlines the relative amount of time that should generally be devoted to each of the *Managing in Reverse* phases, stages, and steps.

	Relative Weight
PHASE I. ASSESSMENT	**50%**
Stage I - Opportunity Analysis	**15%**
Step 1: Measure current performance	10%
Step 2: Establish performance targets	5%
Stage II - Operational Review	**35%**
Step 3: Evaluate underperforming operations	25%
Step 4: Benchmark best practice organizations	10%
PHASE II. IMPLEMENTATION	**50%**
Stage III - Recommendations & implementation	**35%**
Step 5: Recommend operational improvements	10%
Step 6: Implement recommendations	25%
Stage IV - Sustainability & Refinement	**15%**
Step 7: Monitor outcomes	5%
Step 8: Refine improvements	10%

Figure 12: **Relative percentage of time dedicated to each phase, stage, and step of *Managing in Reverse***

CHAPTER SUMMARY: Key Points

1. Step 1 to optimizing performance is to measure the current performance of an operation's outputs, outcomes, or deliverables. Approximately ten percent of a performance improvement project should be devoted to this step.

2. Measuring current performance involves setting up key performance indicators (KPIs) or metrics that track the current and critical outcomes of an operation.

3. The best format for setting up and monitoring KPIs is to track them in a concise, high-level format known as a dashboard. A dashboard shows the basic vital signs of an operation and tells management at a glance how well the operation is performing.

4. Critical outcomes are those that denote the purposes of an operation and also contribute to and align with the business objectives of the overall organization.

5. KPIs should be established for each of the six basic management levels within an organization, including the CEO (and chiefs), presidents, vice presidents, directors, managers, and supervisors.

6. There are eight components of effective KPI dashboards:

    a. KPI dashboards must be succinct and only track the outcomes of an operation that correspond to its primary purposes and objectives.

b. KPIs must be aligned with and contribute to the business objectives (strategy, mission, vision, goals, and values) of the entire organization.

c. KPIs should be tracked in time intervals that allow managers to respond quickly to problems.

d. KPIs must be accurate.

e. Dashboards should contain historical data to reflect performance trends.

f. Dashboards should contain baselines to track improvement.

g. KPIs should include volume drivers.

h. KPIs must include performance targets.

7. There are five primary purposes for establishing KPI dashboards:

a. They are used to conduct operational assessments.

b. They are a management tool.

c. They largely make future, one-time operational assessments unnecessary.

d. They increase productivity.

e. They produce leaner operations.

8. Step 1, as with the other seven steps, must be carried out in some proximity to their relative weight of the overall project. Otherwise, you might devote too much time to a particular step when the goal is to implement and sustain change.

STEP 2

Establish
Performance Targets

PHASE I. ASSESSMENT		
Stage I - Opportunity Analysis		
Step 1: Measure current performance		
Step 2: Establish performance targets		
Stage II - Operational Review		
Step 3: Evaluate underperforming operations		
Step 4: Benchmark best practice organizations		
PHASE II. IMPLEMENTATION		
Stage III - Recommendations & implementation		
Step 5: Recommend operational improvements		
Step 6: Implement recommendations		
Stage IV - Sustainability & Refinement		
Step 7: Monitor outcomes		
Step 8: Refine improvements		

S tep 2 to optimizing performance is to establish performance targets for operational outcomes and calculate the opportunity for improvement. This will determine if and to what extent an operation can be improved. Establishing performance targets typically requires about five percent of the total project time.

Performance targets are the goals, expectations, and requirements that reflect the performance standards and objectives of an operation. Without knowing the target, it is difficult to determine whether current performance is excellent or poor. For instance, suppose a person's temperature is 103° Fahrenheit. This isolated information is arbitrary. However, when compared to the average human temperature—somewhere between 97° and 99° (or the oft-quoted temperature of 98.6°), a 103° temperature means something. The person has a high fever. Likewise, without knowing the performance targets of an operation, it is difficult to tell if an operation is underperforming.

Calculating a performance opportunity is done by taking the difference between actual and expected (or targeted) performance and, when possible, converting the difference into a financial opportunity. Figure 13 illustrates how the opportunity is derived by taking the difference between actual and targeted outputs.

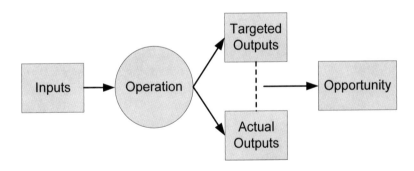

Figure 13: **Outcomes Opportunity**

Perception vs. Reality

Sometimes people perceive that an operation is underperforming and reflects an opportunity for improvement. However, when actual performance is compared against targeted performance, the reality of whether a problem or opportunity exists is revealed and validated. For example, while consulting a medical center on their patient flow and bed management processes, as mentioned in the Preface, medical leadership presumed that delivering mothers on the labor and delivery floor were staying in the hospital far past their allotted forty-eight hours for normal deliveries and ninety-six hours for C-sections. The hospital assumed it was accruing additional costs for caring for these patients longer than medically necessary and that these patients were occupying beds that could have been assigned to new patients.

To determine the legitimacy of the problem, I put on scrubs, rounded with nurses on the maternity floor, and collected discharge data on over 100 patients during a two-week period. After taking the difference between the actual discharge and expected discharge times, I was able to show that new mothers were actually staying in the hospital an average of eight hours less than their allotted time. Because the perception of an existing problem proved wrong, no changes were made to the patient flow process in labor and delivery.

On a different project, this same medical center believed that its radiology department could be operating even more profitably. Radiology had recently improved its profitability by more than sixty percent over the previous year. Nevertheless, hospital administration still felt it was underperforming. Before attempting to improve Radiology's financial performance, I compared its current operating margin to industry best practice benchmark targets. The opportunity calculation showed that the department could still be adding millions more to its bottom line. Based on the benchmarks, we set higher financial performance targets for the radiology department, which were soon achieved.

Accurate Performance Targets

Establishing accurate performance targets can require time and effort, increasing the five percent relative weight of time devoted to this step. However, if targets accurately reflect the right performance goals, the extra effort is worthwhile. Consider, for example, the resources some organizations expend to establish accurate financial budgets. Revenues, costs, volumes, inflationary factors, competitive factors, regulatory factors, and other data are gathered, analyzed, and forecasted to determine the following year's operating income target.

This target becomes the performance target for the entire organization. Each organizational level must work to achieve its individual revenue and cost targets, which contribute to achieving the overall operating income target. Reaching the overall target helps the organization fund its strategic plans and capital investments to keep the organization growing and competitive.

On the other hand, sloppy budgeting, such as setting revenue and cost targets unrealistically too high or too low can be highly problematic for an organization. Targets set too high can demoralize staff and leaders at every level. Targets set too low perpetuate mediocre performance. Soon, no one will take budgets seriously. The overall impact can be severe and put an organization in a precarious position.

Using Benchmarks

Although it takes work to set accurate performance targets, it nevertheless must be done. Performance targets are often derived using internal benchmarks, external benchmarks, or some combination of the two. Internal benchmarks are developed by examining internal performance data and historical trends, environmental and competitive factors, capacity and productivity reports, and other information. External benchmarks can come from the performance data of "best practice" organizations of similar size, industry, geographic region, and other factors. They can also come from associations, industry publications, large financial institutions, and benchmarking companies that maintain large databases of financial, quality, purchasing, productivity, staffing, safety, and other performance data.

While using external benchmarks to set performance targets can be highly valuable, doing so can pose four challenges:

- The first challenge is that internal staff and managers can resist using external benchmarks to create performance targets. Even when benchmark data provide a good comparison, staff may still reject them, claiming their organization is too unique. Sometimes their reasons are justified, sometimes not. For instance, some staff may say that the region of the country in which they operate is unique compared to the benchmark group. Or they will say their products and services are too different, or that the technology they use in production is dissimilar, and so on. Accordingly, staff and managers notoriously reject external benchmark targets. In such cases, senior leadership, particularly the CEO, must decide whether the data is representative and whether the benchmarks should be used to establish performance targets. Without administrative backing, staff may give little credence to newly developed targets based on benchmarks.

- The second challenge is that sometimes benchmark data does not provide a good comparison group. If this is the case, don't use it to set performance targets! While this seems obvious and even silly, I still see large organizations using unsuitable benchmark data for performance targets. This is most frustrating to staff because the intended targets are inaccurate or irrelevant.

- The third challenge is that external benchmarks, even from "best-practice" organizations, may not reflect peak performance. While benchmark data show what other best-practice organizations have accomplished, this does not necessarily mean they have achieved their best performance. Using external benchmarks as performance targets may actually limit an organization from excelling beyond those targets and reaching greater levels of performance.

- The fourth challenge is that external benchmarks can be expensive.

Because of these challenges, it is often important to modify and blend external and internal benchmarks to come up with appropriate performance targets.

Performance Targets on KPI Dashboards

As mentioned in Step 1, once you have established accurate performance targets for a particular operation, you should put them on the operation's KPI dashboard. Adding performance targets to KPI dashboards helps keep management and staff focused on goals and operational outcomes. In addition, by continually tracking variances between current and targeted performance, management and staff are able to identify whether they are on or off track in reaching goals, and to what extent.

Operating statements are a good example of a financial dashboard that shows KPIs, targets, and variances. For instance, operating statements show financial targets in the form of budgeted revenue and cost targets. They also show how current and projected performance are compared to targets. Variances between actual and targeted (budgeted) performance are shown to indicate whether targets are being met or not, and to what degree.

Managers must never take their eyes off the KPIs and performance targets of an operation. While working for a large manufacturing company many years ago, I recall hearing the renowned philanthropist and founder of the company repeatedly say, "Keep your eye on the indicator."

Financial Opportunity

When actual performance is compared to targeted performance, the variance between the two indicates whether an opportunity exists, and to what extent. If an opportunity does exist, it should be converted into a financial opportunity whenever possible. This allows leaders to decide whether the opportunity is worth pursuing, and if so, how much they can spend on improvements to yield an appropriate return on investment. For instance, if you are trying to lower employee turnover from thirty percent to fifteen percent what is that goal worth in financial terms? In calculating this, you would consider certain factors such as recruiting, training, and even downtime costs.

Financial opportunities are often calculated in one of two ways, or a combination of both. The first way impacts the income statement and is based on how operational improvements affect costs and revenues on an annual basis. For instance, if you are able to reduce overtime or employee turnover, how will those affect your annual labor costs? Or, if you increase the pricing of your products and services, how will that affect your annual revenue? These improvements should be calculated on an annual basis since they may be ongoing. However, remember that one dollar of cost savings is equal to one dollar added to the bottom line, whereas one dollar of added revenue only adds a fraction of that amount to the bottom line based on its profit margin. For instance, if a company's profit margin is ten percent, then only 10 cents for each dollar of added revenue transfers to the bottom line.

The second way to calculate a financial opportunity is based on how it impacts your balance sheet, or the organization's assets and liabilities. Often, these operational improvements provide a one-time financial impact. For instance, if inventory levels or accounts receivables are reduced, how will that impact cash? Since these improvements may not recur over time, they may only provide a one-time infusion of cash or reduction in liabilities. Some opportunities broadly impact both the income statement and the balance sheet.

Without calculating a financial opportunity, it is hard to know whether an opportunity is worth pursuing. While consulting a large medical center as a new healthcare consultant years ago, I found it was not billing insurance companies for all the medications it was providing to treat patients. When I discovered this, I initially thought the hospital was losing significant amounts of annual revenue. However, after calculating the financial opportunity of the problem, I found that the difference was negligible. This was because government payers and some insurance companies were reimbursing the hospital at a bundled rate based on a patient's diagnosis. This bundled rate included room charges, medical supplies, x-rays, lab tests, certain nursing procedures, and medications given to the patient. I found that only a very small fraction of the insurance companies reimbursed the hospital for each individual item that was charged, on a fee-for-service or percentage-of-charge basis. Transforming the pharmacy billing process to ensure every medication was charged was too insignificant an opportunity to further pursue.

This leads to the question: How does an organization determine if a particular opportunity is worth pursuing? The answer depends on the return on investment. Other factors are also considered, such as the size of the financial opportunity relative to the size of the institution, its financial situation, the difficulty of implementing the solution, the priority of other improvement projects, and so on. For a smaller company, it may be worth prioritizing a $100,000 opportunity; whereas, for a much larger organization, a $500,000 opportunity may be secondary to other larger, more critical opportunities. This will be discussed further in Step 5, Recommend Operational Improvements. At this point, however, it is time to discuss how to pinpoint problems and opportunities for improvement in an organization.

Top-Down Analysis

From massive organizations to small business units, the method for identifying poorly performing operations and improvement opportunities is the same. That method is to conduct a top-down analysis at the highest operational level, then drill down from there to the next operational level, and to the next until poorly performing operations are ultimately identified (see Figure 14).

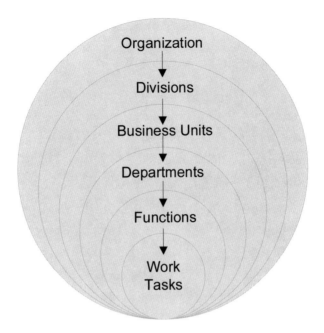

Figure 14: **Top-down analysis**

For example, by looking at an organization's consolidated income statement, suppose that it is operating in the red. This simply means that somewhere, financial targets are not being met. To understand what operational improvements should be made to correct the problems, specific operations responsible for missing their financial targets must be identified. This is how a turnaround project is conducted. At the highest level, you review each line item on the consolidated operating statement to identify general problems at the organizational level.

Next, you drill down to the divisional-level to further isolate the problems by reviewing the line items of their respective operating statements. As each division's operating statements are examined, the divisions causing the most overall operational problems are singled out.

Problems are further defined and isolated by delving into the underperforming divisions' business units. Underperforming business units are similarly singled out, by reviewing their current-to-targeted performance on their respective operating statements. After identifying the problematic business units, you drill down further by reviewing the operating statements for each of the business units' departments. This top-down analysis will help you pinpoint the exact areas not meeting their financial targets. Once you have singled out the underperforming departments, you can begin to look at the functional areas and work tasks to determine the root causes of the problems.

The same exercise would apply to any operational metric you are tracking. For instance, reviewing quality indicators, customer service, throughput, employee turnover, sales, and other metrics starts with the KPI dashboard at the highest operational level. You then drill down to the KPI dashboards of the lower operational levels one-by-one. Once underperforming operations are identified by comparing actual to targeted performance and financial opportunities are calculated, the real fun begins—the operational review conducted in Step 3.

CHAPTER SUMMARY: Key Points

1. Step 2 to optimizing performance is to establish performance targets for the outputs, outcomes, or deliverables of an operation and calculate the improvement opportunity. Approximately five percent of a performance improvement project is dedicated to this step.

2. To calculate a performance opportunity, take the difference between actual and targeted performance.

3. Comparing actual to targeted performance shows the reality of a perceived problem or opportunity.

4. Performance targets often come from either internal or external benchmarks, or some combination of the two. Using external benchmarks in conjunction with internal benchmarks is the best way to establish performance targets since using external benchmarks alone can pose four challenges:

   - Because staff may believe their organization is so unique, they can still resist using external benchmarks to establish targets—even when good comparison benchmark data is used. In response, it is critical that senior leadership, particularly the CEO, back the decision to use external benchmark data to establish performance targets.

   - Sometimes, external benchmark data do not provide a good comparison group. If so, do not use the data to set performance targets.

- External benchmarks may not reflect peak performance.

- External benchmarks can be expensive.

5. KPI dashboards should include performance targets so that variances are easily tracked.

6. When operational opportunities are discovered, they should be converted into financial opportunities, whenever possible. This will help leaders determine if the opportunity is worth pursuing and how much can be invested to realize the benefit.

7. From massive organizations to small companies, the method for identifying poorly performing operations is the same. It is based on conducting a top-down analysis by reviewing the KPIs at the highest operational level and then drilling down to the KPIs at the next operational level until specific operational problems and opportunities are identified.

STEP 3

Evaluate Underperforming Operations

PHASE I. ASSESSMENT
Stage I - Opportunity Analysis
Step 1: Measure current performance
Step 2: Establish performance targets
Stage II - Operational Review
Step 3: Evaluate underperforming operations
Step 4: Benchmark best practice organizations
PHASE II. IMPLEMENTATION
Stage III - Recommendations & implementation
Step 5: Recommend operational improvements
Step 6: Implement recommendations
Stage IV - Sustainability & Refinement
Step 7: Monitor outcomes
Step 8: Refine improvements

S tep 3 is evaluating underperforming operations to identify specific problems and opportunities for improvement. This step requires about twenty-five percent of the total project time. Once underperforming operations have been identified in Steps 1 and 2, it is necessary to pinpoint the causes of underperformance so proper solutions can be recommended and implemented. To achieve this, it is time to move backwards, "managing in reverse," from the outputs of an operation to the operation itself, and then, to its inputs (see Figure 15). If multiple underperforming operations have been identified from the opportunity analysis, they should be ranked and prioritized based on their respective opportunities.

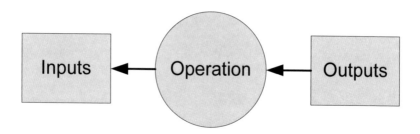

Figure 15: **Managing in Reverse** from the
outputs to the operation and its inputs

The method for evaluating an underperforming operation follows a list of eight sequential tasks, which will be discussed below. These tasks are designed to assess the current state of an operation and consider both the tangible, nonhuman components and the intangible, human components. The goal of the assessment is to determine the root causes of problems or improvement opportunities. Once you identify these causes, summarize them in a *Findings Report*, which is used to develop appropriate solutions and improvement recommendations. When listing your findings, make sure they are specific, as general findings are too vague to be useful when developing recommendations. For instance, stating that an operation "has fragmented or redundant processes causing inefficiencies," or that "there is a lack of accountability and ownership causing low productivity" is unhelpful information unless you also identify specific processes with supporting examples and data.

During this discovery process, it is critical that you simultaneously seek potential solutions while working through each of the eight tasks. These potential solutions will be used in Step 5 when operational improvements are finalized and recommended. While you interview administrators, managers, vendors, customers, frontline staff, and other stakeholders about underperforming operations, be sure to ask them how they would improve it. Actively seek their feedback and document it for later use. Most veteran consultants recognize that many solutions for improving operations will come from within the organization. Some of the best solutions will likely come from the front-line employees who live and breathe the operation each day.

Sometimes, staff will disclose very sensitive information that can reflect the real cause of operational problems, such as leadership problems. In these cases, assure them that whatever they disclose will be held in confidence, and keep those confidences. In fact, if you are trustworthy and not pretentious, employees will disclose operational problems rather quickly. They often know how to fix the problems as well. In these cases, be sure to recognize employees for the information they provide. Unfortunately, I've seen too many consultants take credit for others' input.

Also, during the operational review process, it is common to quickly discover important solutions that can easily be implemented. In these cases, don't wait for reports, analyses, and presentations to be completed before implementing them. Get the necessary approvals so the recommendations can be quickly implemented and operations improved.

Getting to the Truth

Before exploring the eight sequential tasks of evaluating the current state of an operation, it is important to first set the stage for Step 3. In essence, Step 3 requires getting to the truth of a problem or the heart of an opportunity. Only after the truth has been unearthed can you make precise recommendations that address the problems. Without discovering the truth, recommendations are at best, hit-or-miss educated guesses that may or may not provide optimal solutions. This concept is tantamount to a physician who must first correctly diagnose a patient's health problem before prescribing the correct path to recovery.

Correctly diagnosing the problem or identifying the opportunity of an operation is a highly qualitative exercise, interspersed with data gathering and analysis. However, because of the qualitative nature of Step 3, it requires a shift in approach from the highly quantitative exercises of Steps 1 and 2. This shift actually makes many managers, consultants, and teams leave their comfort zones. Step 3 necessitates that they largely leave behind the security of their spreadsheets and computer monitors in order to integrate into the operation—its culture, people, leadership, processes, environment, systems, and so forth. It's like walking down from the stands of an arena onto the basketball court to experience how the game is really played.

It's a whole different reality when you are on the court, feeling the intimidation of a six-foot-nine-inches tall, 260-pound Goliath vaulting over the top of you and crushing the ball through the net, or feeling the infusion of adrenaline as the home crowd roars with thunder after a steal, followed by an amazing alley-oop. But this is where the current state of an operation—the human and the non-human elements—is really discovered—at court level, with a jersey on—a place where data, calculators, and spreadsheets don't perform so well.

Ironically, too many leaders, consultants, and teams never roll up their sleeves and fully immerse themselves in an operation to make the kinds of discoveries that can impact performance the most. Yet they still make improvement recommendations despite having never played the game nor even observed it at the court level.

I recall an instance wherein a group of internal consultants at a large health system recommended that all orthopedic surgeons use the same knee implants to cut costs. Although the recommendation was approved by administration, it quickly backfired. One surgeon told me that there was no way he was going to change devices after having been trained in his residency to use a certain knee implant, which had great outcomes. He said he would take his cases to a different hospital before changing implants so that the health system could save money. He had been using knee implants from the same vendor for many years. He also had close ties with the medical device rep who brought the knee implants into each surgical case. The rep would scrub in and help the surgeon in the operating room fit each patient. The two had become close friends and even went on vacations together with their families. The surgeon was simply not going to change implants, nor would he change his surgical implant rep.

Understanding the impact of a recommendation from this perspective requires much more than making a few cost calculations in some back office. To really understand the current operation, the consultants should have put on scrubs, observed cases in the operating room, talked to the surgeons, listened to their feedback, and felt the stress of surgery. However, this would have required consultants to venture into unfamiliar territory with unfamiliar people.

Because this step can be a bit daunting, many either ignore it altogether or do the bare minimum by conducting interviews with senior leadership, managers, vendors, and possibly customers in an attempt to dissect operational problems. However, while important, such interviews are insufficient for discovering core problems and opportunities. Holding such interviews is like obtaining information about a football game from a blimp flying over a football stadium. This 1,000-foot "eye in the sky" aerial view is not the same as getting on the field and playing the game.

Gaining that frontline perspective can be a little frightening at first, especially if you've never played the game or know little about it. For instance, years ago, I arrived at my very first hospital consulting project. When I got to the hospital, my boss (the acting COO of the hospital) told me, "Go fix admitting and the emergency departments." That was all the instruction I received. I really had no idea what the admitting department even was, as my only hospital experiences consisted of visiting family or friends who were patients. When I found the admission department, I had to ask a registration clerk behind a counter what the department did and what its functions were. Little did they know that I was responsible for improving it.

When I got to the emergency department, my tail was really between my legs as I saw sick patients crowded in the waiting room, security guards with handguns, emergency medical technicians wheeling patients from ambulances into the emergency room, helicopter flight teams rushing patients to trauma rooms, and physicians and nurses scurrying from room to room. As I stuck out like a sore thumb in my starched white shirt and tie, the last thing I wanted was for one of the physicians or nurses to stop and ask me what I was doing there.

I quickly realized I was either going to sink or swim and needed to roll up my sleeves and jump in—the same as I had done with consulting projects in other industries that I was initially unfamiliar with. In an unassuming manner, I integrated into the department, made friends with the staff, and asked for their help to learn the operations. The project was successful. In fact, some years later, I was being flown across the United States, consulting emergency room medical directors and nursing directors about their operations and showing them how they could be more efficient, reduce costs, generate more revenue, and improve patient satisfaction.

You should know that getting to the truth of a problem or the heart of an opportunity can be met with heavy resistance. You can be quite unpopular when evaluating an operation. While some leaders are helpful and open their doors to an operational review by providing support and carte blanche access to data, people, and systems, others are openly resentful and meet you with intense opposition. Often, this is because getting to the truth can be like performing detective work on the sacred ground of a territorial or antagonistic manager or executive. In these cases, interpersonal finesse, composure, perceptiveness, and perseverance are required as you carefully peel back the layers of the operational onion.

Many leaders simply don't want someone in their area who may uncover intentional or unintentional leadership blemishes that could make them feel vulnerable and threatened. Some leaders naturally react defensively or with hostility as they criticize, oppose, and undermine the person or team reviewing their operation. Other managers are just plain tired of consultants showing up and not producing results. Managers can also be petulant just because they have to devote more time to yet another consultant. And some are just proud and eager to show you what you don't know, try to intimidate you, and hope you will go away. Regardless of the reasons for resistance, you can do four things to help mitigate it.

- First, obtain authorization and the backing of the senior executive sponsoring the project before beginning an operational review. Otherwise, going into an operational review can be like walking into a lion's den.

- Second, request that the sponsoring executive notify all pertinent layers of management about the review. The executive should introduce the project and clearly state its purpose, which is to optimize operational outcomes. They should also outline the eight steps involved in the review; introduce the person or team conducting the review, ask the management team for their support and access to data, people, and systems, provide a start date and an estimated end date for the review, and ask the management team to inform their staff about the project so they are prepared for inquiries.

- Third, inform the sponsoring executive that he or she should anticipate some opposition to the project from both the management team and the staff—even from esteemed colleagues. Getting to the heart of an opportunity or problem can be like performing surgery, where cutting through the tissue can be painful, but nevertheless a requisite process to diagnosing underlying problems. And although grunts and groans are certainly expected, it doesn't mean that some anesthetic can't be applied to help everyone get through the process. Sometimes the best anesthetic is to listen to concerns and show empathy while still leading with composure, optimism, and a firm resolve.

I have consulted on improvement projects where the directors of underperforming operations were close friends with the executives who hired me. On one such project, a director over a particular department I was reviewing had convinced the executive who hired me that I didn't know what I was doing, and that I was going about the project in the wrong way. One late evening, after the two of them met, the executive over the project overreacted, paged me on an overhead speaker system, and asked me to come to his office. When I arrived, he angrily demanded, "What are you doing in that department?"

I reminded the executive of our prior conversation, wherein I told him he should expect to see emotional reactions from some management and staff just because I showed up in their areas. I also reminded him of our agreement that he would back me until the review was complete. I then reassured him that I was always very courteous, congenial, and professional. He calmed down, and I was able to finish my review. After the review, I showed him my findings, which indicated years of negligent management and extreme financial losses. He removed the director.

I have experienced many similar projects where poorly performing executives nearly sabotaged an operational review by trying to turn the CEO against me or my entire team of consultants—whom the CEO had hired. In the end, some of these executives also lost their jobs after information emerged about how poorly they were running their respective areas. Conversely, high-performing leaders typically welcome an operational review, engage themselves in the process, and partner with the person or team conducting the review.

- Fourth, before beginning an operational review, you should first interview the management team overseeing the operation. You should also interview other key stakeholders (i.e., organizational leadership, board members, investors, vendors, and customers). The purpose of conducting these interviews is to build relationships, gain support for the project, and glean valuable information and insight into the operational problems and opportunities. Seasoned managers and stakeholders usually know where problems exist as well as potential solutions. This can save considerable time during the review process.

In addition, the information stakeholders share about an operation will provide an excellent overview of the operation's objectives, processes, systems, staffing, leadership, and other areas, making the operation easier to understand and less complex. This information can also help determine if the outcomes of the operation are aligned with the overall organization's objectives.

TASK 1

DETERMINE IF THE OPERATION SHOULD EXIST

The first task in reviewing an operation is to answer the question of whether the operation under review should even exist or if it should be shut down or sold off. Usually, the answer to this question is immediately obvious. Sometimes, however, it is not and requires a more extensive operational review before the question can be answered. Either way, it should be answered as soon as possible so valuable resources aren't consumed improving an operation that should be discontinued.

It may be readily apparent that a particular operation should be eliminated if it is losing large sums of money and is not aligned with and does not contribute to the overall objectives of the organization (i.e., the organization's strategic plan, mission, vision, goals, and values). On the other hand, a poorly performing operation, that is integral to the larger organization and is aligned with its business objectives, should continue, but may need to be transformed or even outsourced to provide greater efficiency.

At one organization I consulted, the decision was made to divest an operation because it did not have the customer volume base to make it profitable. The decision was made to sell it. At another organization, it wasn't until most of the eight operational review tasks were completed that we could determine that a particular operation had to be eliminated. It had been so poorly managed for so many years that we finally determined it was at a point of no return and needed to be shut down. In both cases, neither operation really contributed to the business objectives of their organization.

Operations that do not contribute to the primary purpose of the organization not only devour resources but can hinder the performance of the overall organization. This is because well-performing operations must compensate and financially offset poorly performing operations. Large organizations with subsidiary companies, or business units, must recognize that if any are losing money, they must be turned around or shut down. Yet it is surprising to watch organizations continue to allow poorly performing business units and product lines continue to eat up the profits of other, well-performing operations.

I once consulted with a large hospitality organization that fully understood this concept. When the organization had modified its business plan, they wanted to ensure that each of the divisions contributed to the newly formed goals and strategy of the organization. However, because one division was no longer in alignment with the new business plan, administration decided to divest it rather than transform it. The price tag of the divestiture was over $1 billion. My role was to facilitate the corporate restructuring caused by this elimination.

On a much smaller scale, I was hired to resuscitate a financial organization. While reviewing several of the core departments, I found a manager in one department spending all his time building snazzy computer programs and databases that had nothing to do with the objectives of the department or organization. At first, the manager tried to dazzle me by showing me his sophisticated computer creations. Not being fooled, I quickly realized that all his time and effort was counterproductive because his personal projects were out of scope with the purposes of the department. This small, functional-level operation needed to be discontinued. As my operational review continued, I later found that about one-third of the department was excess fat that needed trimming. After my review, we let the director, the manager, and one-third of the department go. This scenario demonstrated that when the leader of an operation is not aligned with the business objectives of the overall organization, much of their department follows suit.

TASK 2

REVIEW THE
ORGANIZATIONAL STRUCTURE

After determining whether an operation should continue to exist, the next task is to review the organizational structure. As previously mentioned, an operation is composed of two separate, though interwoven, infrastructures—the human component and the nonhuman component. However, because non-human processes, such as computer systems, equipment, facilities, procedures, and so forth, are governed by human beings, it is essential to first review the human component.

On the other hand, if you were creating a new operation, you would begin with the non-human, tangible component of the operation (i.e., processes, computer systems, equipment, facilities, procedures, and so forth). After this infrastructure was designed, you would next develop the critical human components (i.e., organizational chart, leadership, staff, culture, etc.) to manage the operation. But in an established operation where you are optimizing performance, you would work in the reverse manner, looking first at the human component and then at the non-human component. And it begins with the organizational chart.

Some might debate that assessing leadership is the next most important step, which is Task 3. However, if an organizational chart is defective, it can pose a host of problems for any leader and be a deterrent to good operational outcomes. An effective organization chart, on the other hand, helps leaders perform at higher levels by facilitating better staff accountability, organizational collaboration and communication, speed and efficiency, quality control, customer service, and employee satisfaction. Once the right organizational chart is in place, it is time to make sure the right leaders are in place.

With that said, the best way to build an optimal organizational chart is to begin at the highest management level of the operation you are reviewing. If you are improving the performance of an entire organization, you would start at the chief-level, and construct the right positions at the top. In building out this leadership level, as with all management levels, you would start with a blank sheet of paper and diagram the right positions, which would oversee the next management level down. Names should not be included in order to be objective.

Assuming that no changes would be made with the CEO, he or she would review and modify the chief-level of leadership as necessary. The current chiefs would not be involved in building out this top level of management since some of their positions might need to be altered, merged, or eliminated. In fact, this is the time to propose leadership changes during the organizational chart review process. Once the chief-level is complete, you move down to the next level, and then to the next, until all management levels have been reviewed and changes proposed.

The ideal process for completing each management level, one at a time, would be that once the top level of management—the chief level—has been reviewed and changes proposed, you would then fulfill the proposed changes and appoint the right leaders in each position. You would then use the newly appointed chief level to help construct the next management level down, the president level—those whom the chiefs would oversee. After the president-level has been reviewed and modified, you would use them to help build the next management layer down—the vice president-level. This process would be repeated through each management level, down to the managers and supervisors.

At the final level, you would build out the frontline staff positions with the help of managers and supervisors. The managers and supervisors would also help determine the right number of staff they need for each functional area. Once the proposed organizational chart is complete and each position is filled, the new chart will show the correct job titles and employee names.

The Process of Improving Organizational Charts

Fortunately, the process for reviewing and appropriately modifying an organizational chart is straightforward and may be simpler than you think if you are following the right approach. The first step in the process is to get current organizational charts and employee data from Human Resources for the operation you are assessing. However, don't be surprised if an organization does not have current organizational charts. More often than not, Human Resources, as well as leaders over poorly performing operations, do not maintain updated organizational charts. In these cases, new charts must be created.

While consulting a large, underperforming manufacturing company, I asked Human Resources for the current organizational charts of their entire company. As suspected, Human Resources did not keep updated organizational charts, and neither did most of the leadership, for that matter. However, after getting an employee dataset from Human Resources, I was able to produce nearly 200 current organization charts. These charts accounted for every employee in the entire organization, which consisted of several thousand people.

When you need to create current organizational charts, the employee data set will help you build them. This data should include the following fields of information: employee name, employee ID number, hire date, direct supervisor, department number, department name, location, job title, job grade, and full-time equivalent (FTE). In fact, this data will not only help you build current organizational charts but will also help you reconstruct them in the right way. Be sure to analyze the data since it can provide important insights about the organization and how the layout should be constructed. For example, use the data to show the following information:

- Number of employees by department or cost center

- Number of employees by manager (all leadership positions)

- Number of employees by location

- Number of job titles

- Number of employees by job title

- Number of managers with direct reports

- Number of managers with just one direct report, two director reports, etc.

- Number of managers with no direct reports

- Number of leadership employees

- Total headcount

- Total full-time equivalents

- Average span of control overall and by department

- Average years of service overall and by department, location, and manager

Once you have the employee data and current organizational charts in hand, you can next review the following six components see where changes need to be made:

1. Functional alignment
2. Management levels
3. Spans of control
4. Job titles
5. Cost centers and budgets
6. Physical layout

As you review each of these six components, start to outline the proposed organizational charts one level of management at a time, beginning at the top.

1. Functional Alignment. Arguably, the most important component of an effective organizational structure is the functional alignment of operations and their suboperations under single managers. (I use the word "manager" loosely throughout the book to refer to all leadership positions, including chiefs, presidents, vice presidents, directors, managers, and supervisors.) When functions are not aligned under a single manager but are split between two or more, the results are confusion, frustration, communication problems, fragmentation, inconsistent processes and outcomes, and a lack of ownership.

The reason for these outcomes is that when similar functions are not aligned under the same manager, the operation naturally splits into a number of pieces equal to the number of managers overseeing it. For instance, if there are three directors over one particular function, the function will eventually divide into three parts because leaders run things differently. Leaders have varying styles, strengths, weaknesses, performance expectations, expertise, priorities, interpersonal skills, and so forth, which not only cause operations to be governed differently but also cause employees to gravitate toward the leader they like most. Consequently, operations divide, and outcomes become uneven and consequently substandard. Though the objectives for each of the three directors are still the same, each will vary in how they drive the outcomes of their operations.

At a large health system with multiple hospitals and a large number of physician clinics, I found that the patient registration processes, involving some 200 employees, were overseen by fourteen different directors. The problem was that these fourteen directors did not report to a common registration leader who oversaw the overall process. As a result, there were basically fourteen different registration processes.

In the same health system, the billing department was split in half and overseen by two different directors. Because two different directors ran the entire billing operation, animosity arose between the two groups of employees. In fact, the directors and their managers became outright hostile to each other. The two groups differed in wages, work schedules, billing and collection procedures, performance expectations, and technology. At one point, the staffs of the two directors were not allowed to talk to each other. Both groups felt things were unfair between them. Consequently, morale was low, employee performance was poor, the medical center lost millions of dollars each year in uncollected claims, costs were high, and employee turnover was high. This was an easy fix. We placed billing under one director.

While functional alignment is the best organizational chart design—where the same functions ultimately reside under a single leader—there are cases where a matrixed organizational chart composed of solid and dotted reporting lines is advantageous. A matrixed chart is where certain employees may report to both a primary manager, reflected on the organizational chart by a solid line, and a secondary manager, reflected by a dotted line. This is often beneficial when an employee primarily reports to their functional leader but also reports to another leader based on the employee's primary location.

For instance, an organization may have its marketing department centrally located at company headquarters. However, the organization may also need to place marketing managers in business units located in different states or countries. In these cases, the marketing managers located outside company headquarters should still functionally report to a corporate marketing director with a solid line. However, the marketing managers may also need to have a dotted line—a secondary reporting relationship—with the business unit directors of their respective locations. This would be helpful when locations have different customer demographics, laws, product lines, and marketing strategies. A dotted reporting line would facilitate better collaboration between business unit directors and marketing managers. And since the business unit director is responsible for the outcomes of his or her business unit, he or she would want to have some influence and control over marketing.

The easiest way to review functional alignment is to look at current organizational charts and identify employees who perform the same functions. It might even be helpful to color-code the positions on the organizational charts that represent the same functions. Different colors can be used for each functional area. At the end of this exercise, you might find a hodgepodge of different colors scattered across organizational charts with less uniformity than you had expected. If this is the case, you may have identified one of the biggest problems of the entire operation.

The next step is to develop a proposed organizational chart in which like colors or functions, are aligned under the same supervisor, manager, director, or vice president. Comparing these current and proposed color-coded organizational charts side-by-side is a powerful way to illuminate the disarray and seek approval for restructuring departments. When functions are realigned under single managers, you may find the need to consolidate managers and staff positions, resulting in cost savings.

2. Management Levels. The next step is to review the hierarchy, or number of management levels. Organizations operating with fewer layers of management run more efficiently than those with many layers. Fewer layers of management in the chain of command will translate into faster decision-making, quicker response times, more efficient and direct communication, increased managerial accountability, and lower management labor costs. Staying with the basic six levels of management hierarchy (CEO and chiefs, presidents, vice presidents, directors, managers, and supervisors) can be quite efficient because this standard of hierarchy is well-understood and a clearly delineated model. While some instances necessitate using off-standard titles such as senior vice president, administrative director, senior manager, coordinator, etc., typically adding more management layers dilutes accountability, hinders efficiency, and adds labor costs. At one company I consulted, it was common for even their smaller departments to have an executive director, a senior director, a director, a senior manager, a manager II, and a manager! Six levels of management in a small department such as this negatively impact operational effectiveness.

3. Span of Control. The next component of reviewing an organizational chart is to look at the managerial spans of control, or the number of people directly reporting to a manager (or a president, vice president, director, manager, or supervisor). Optimal spans of control typically range from eight to twelve direct reports for all levels of leadership. While having more than twelve direct reports may place too many demands on a manager, fewer than eight may mean the organization is top heavy, with too many management positions. Nonetheless, fewer than eight direct reports can be justified when a department does not require a large number of staff, such as a small legal, purchasing, or compliance department, or when a manager must commit a significant portion of his or her time to performing specialized duties. In addition, some professionals requiring no staff at all may justify a managerial title based on the importance of their position and their need for credibility with customers, vendors, or government agencies. Some refer to these management positions as "individual contributors."

4. Job Titles. While perhaps not as essential as the other items on this list, job titles do play an important role in creating a well-defined organization chart. In one organization, I found nearly 1,500 different job titles. There was little uniformity in the nomenclature used for the job titles throughout the company. This posed problems with the various management levels, pay grades, and job responsibilities. Soon, job titles had very little meaning or value and caused much confusion. Not only couldn't you tell what an employee did based on their job title, but you weren't certain about what management level they really were at. Directors reported to managers, and vice versa. Each time a leader wanted to give an employee a pay raise, the leader would just change the employee's job title and submit a request to human resources.

The fewer the job titles and the more standardized they are, the easier it is to functionally align staff and reduce the number of management levels in an organization. Job titles should also match job descriptions. So, some of your work may include rewriting job descriptions to finalize an ideal organizational chart. And while some organizations use job titles as a career ladder for nearly every position, such as Buyer I, II, and III, other organizations avoid doing so to keep titles simple, clean, and concise.

5. Cost Centers and Budgets. Once the functional alignment, management levels, spans of control, and job titles are reviewed, it is imperative that you connect the organizational chart to cost centers and budgets. The key is to ensure that leadership oversees the right cost centers and budgets to which they are accountable. If two directors share a budget, no one is accountable for setting and managing it. If a director has control over all his or her managers' budgets, then the managers are not accountable—only the director. Managers must be involved in budget setting and budget management over their respective areas if they are to perform at expected levels. They must know the revenue and costs of the operations they manage. Otherwise, they really aren't managing, and their job titles should be downgraded. Managers, by definition, manage and should be held accountable for the finances of the operation they oversee.

In addition, be sure to make a list of all cost centers by manager at every level of the organization. The list may indicate that a particular executive has far too many departments to effectively oversee. This would be a good time to more evenly divide cost centers, merge some, or eliminate some, so long as functional alignment is preserved.

6. Physical Layout. Finally, an organizational chart review must take into consideration the locations where employees reside. Some organizational charts are very complex because of the staff's geography. A physical layout showing where staff are located helps put an organizational chart into a more workable perspective. For instance, based on staff locale (including remote staff), the management structure may need some adjustment to ensure better oversight of critical offsite areas. In addition, analyzing an organization's physical layout helps trigger pertinent questions about whether locations are staffed appropriately. Some locations could be overstaffed while others are understaffed, based on the various work loads and production volumes at different sites.

TASK 3

EVALUATE THE LEADERSHIP AND THEIR COMPENSATION

Once you have reviewed the organizational structure to find opportunities for operational improvement, you will need to assess the leadership. While assessing leadership is third on the list of these eight sequential tasks, it is the most crucial. Poor leadership is arguably the most common reason for operational underperformance. This is because poor leadership affects both the human and non-human components of an operation, which directly impact outcomes. Poor leaders can cost an organization millions of dollars or even sink an operation altogether.

Interestingly, the attitude, style, personality, expectations, expertise, and behaviors of a leader cascade throughout an operation. Over time, a leader's staff becomes a fairly homogenous group, adopting the characteristics, performance behaviors, and expectations of their leader. For instance, have you ever observed a department or even an entire organization that possessed a distinct personality or reputation that seemed to resemble the characteristics of its leader? I once worked for a mid-sized manufacturing company that had a reputation for caring for its employees, giving back to the community, and producing high quality, handmade products. The founder of the organization was that kind of man. He was generous and compassionate to his employees and took pride in the work of his company. Employees loved him and loved working for him. And they seemed to reflect his qualities.

After the founder died, the new leadership changed the way the organization was run. Much of the company's previous identity and reputation changed as well, reflecting the new leadership's style and philosophy. New services were added, wages were capped, handmade processes were replaced with automation, and profitability appeared to be the priority. These changes weren't necessarily good or bad, just different, as they seemed to reflect the distinctive manner of the new leadership. Over time, the culture of the organization shifted as well, adopting the characteristics of the new leaders.

I also worked in senior leadership for an organization in which the accounting department was known for being uncooperative and unfriendly. After meeting the CFO, I immediately identified the source of the department's reputation. This person was uncooperative and unfriendly. In the same organization, a second department was known for its hostility toward employees outside its department. Once again, after meeting that department's vice president, it was easy to associate the entire department's hostility with its leader.

The poor attributes of a leader trickle down and affect not only the staff but also the outcomes of the operation. In the accounting department described above, month-end reports were often late because other departments were not motivated to submit their month-end financial information to the accounting department on time. The second department referred to above was losing millions of dollars because it operated independently and isolated itself from the assistance and collaboration of other departments.

Departments and even entire organizations tend to adopt the traits of their leaders in four ways:

- First, staff whose personalities and styles differ from their leader's will eventually become frustrated and quit. For instance, while high-performing staff will leave a department that is run by a low-performing leaders, conversely, low-performing staff will leave a department that is run by a high-performing leader.

- Second, leaders will "manage out" staff who do not adapt to the leader's style. In fact, not only will high-performing leaders manage out low-performing staff, but low-performing leaders also force out high-performing staff.

- Third, a leader will fill vacant positions with new employees who reflect his or her own attributes and characteristics. An intelligent, productive leader will recruit intelligent, productive employees. Likewise, complacent leaders recruit complacent employees, and honest leaders recruit honest staff.

- Fourth, a leader will influence, support, and expect staff to adopt his or her behaviors. If a leader is hostile, he or she will influence and support that behavior. On the other hand, a leader with integrity will demand integrity from her employees.

Over time, an entire operation will consist of a fairly homogenous group of employees who reflect the attributes, qualities, and characteristics of its leader. When this occurs, the non-human components of an operation, such as the processes, systems, equipment, tools, and facilities, as well as the inputs to the operation, are managed by this consistent set of staff. If the staff is made up of low performers, the non-human components and inputs of the operation will be run poorly and complacently, causing poor outcomes. If the staff is composed of high performers, then the non-human components and inputs of the operation are managed tightly and proficiently, resulting in excellent outcomes.

While state-of-the-art technology can cause impressive outcomes, preeminent outcomes come only from great leadership. Even with state-of-the-art technology, poor leaders cannot fully leverage an operation to produce optimal outcomes. For instance, the best driver in the hands of a poor golfer cannot drive a golf ball the same distance that Tiger Woods could drive a golf ball using a second-rate driver. However, it is fascinating that exemplary leaders, even without state-of-the-art tools and technology, can leverage their resources to produce remarkable outcomes.

And unlike poor leaders, it is interesting that great leaders seldom complain about their equipment, systems, facilities, and so forth. They simply maximize the outcomes the best they can, given their resources. On the other hand, poor leaders tend to blame their people, facilities, computer systems, operational inputs, etc. for poor operational outcomes because they lack the ability to produce stellar results with what they have. Just as a superior football coach will take an average team to great heights, a poor football coach will blame his losses on his team, poor equipment, or bad calls made by referees.

So, how do you evaluate leaders? Following are six ways to distinguish great leaders from poor:

1. First, evaluate the outcomes or the deliverables of the operation a leader oversees. If the deliverables—in terms of cost, quality, revenue, timeliness, employee turnaround, volumes, productivity, customer satisfaction, and so forth—meet or exceed performance targets (which you set in Step 2), you probably have a great leader. The first indication of a poor leader is poor deliverables. Great leaders deliver outstanding, sustained results, just as a great head football coach has an excellent win-loss record.

2. Evaluate the trends of the outcomes to see if they improve or decline. Performance trends may indicate that targets will soon be met, although current performance may fall below expectations. This may be the result of a great leader inheriting a poor operation that he or she is turning around. Performance trends may also indicate the steady decline of an operation, even if it was once exceeding targets. This may be the result of a poor leader inheriting a superior operation that is now deteriorating.

3. Assess the culture. Are the employees happy, productive, motivated, recognized for high performance, and focused on meeting the objectives of the operation and the overall business objectives of the organization? A good working culture that spawns high performance is created by a great leader. The best way to assess the culture is to integrate yourself into the operation through shadowing, interviewing, and observing employees. When getting a feel for the culture, it is most revealing to find out whether employees are encouraged and free to openly communicate their ideas and frustrations, even about their leader. For instance, are the employees psychologically safe? Are employees mentored and developed? Are they empowered to excel in their work, make decisions, and flourish on their own? If not, staff are probably being micromanaged or not managed.

In either case, employees who are not recognized, empowered, accountable, or psychologically safe will lack fulfillment and have a hard time producing optimal outcomes. Furthermore, because they lack a sense of ownership, they often become demoralized and unproductive and merely work for a paycheck. Micromanagers are poor leaders because they don't trust their employees, don't know how to leverage them into producing results, and don't know how to gain a following. These leaders keep their employees down and discouraged rather than inspired. Micromanagers can also come across as self-important, as they believe they have all the answers and take all the credit. Micromanagement, or tightly controlled top-down management, limits the performance of employees and the operation because there is no synergy.

4. Observe how the leader responds to the scrutiny of his or her operation. Is the leader closed, defensive, or annoyed? Great leaders typically welcome scrutiny because they are team players and want to achieve the best results possible. As a result, they are free with their data, provide support when their staff is interviewed, and will show you around the physical operation. They are typically open and friendly to expert help and a sound methodology. I once conducted a performance improvement project in the pharmacy department of a top hospital system. At the outset of the project, the director invited our team into his department and offered us open access to his people, data, systems, and whatever resources we needed to find and make improvements. In fact, he had invited us to see his inpatient and outpatient operations before we even had time to request a tour. Not surprisingly, the human component of his operation was in textbook order, which made our work much easier—updating computer systems and automating pharmaceutical storage and retrieval processes.

Keep in mind that even great leaders may initially be reluctant to lend as much support to an improvement project as this pharmacy director did. This may be due to a long history of repetitive performance reviews that have yielded no improvement.

Conversely, the pharmacy director at another top medical system was visibly angry when I entered his shop. He would not open his operations and data to me until he was compelled to by senior leadership. Not coincidentally, his pharmacy operations had significant opportunities.

5. Observe whether the leader blames the systems, facilities, equipment, tools, and inputs for poor outcomes. Some leaders can persuasively communicate that the nonhuman components and inputs of their operations are responsible for poor outcomes. They often hide behind these as scapegoats for the real problem—themselves. These leaders often convince administrations to invest more money in technology and capital equipment to improve operations, which may only yield marginal gains after implementation.

While systems may need to be updated, the key is to first determine whether existing systems have been leveraged to their maximum capacity. In addition, it is wise to use benchmarking to see if other organizations that employ the same systems are experiencing good operational outcomes. Answering these questions will help determine whether systems, equipment, and facilities are truly antiquated, unable to deliver targeted outcomes, and need to be replaced. If not, the leader may need to be replaced.

Once, I consulted an organization where the accounts receivable in a particular department had spiraled out of control. The director of the department had blamed her billing system for the problem and convinced administration to purchase an expensive new system to correct the problem. Just before the purchase, I urged administration to hold off until I had completed my review of the department. I found that the department was in complete disarray. I then benchmarked twenty other similar best-practice organizations, where I found that ten were using the very same accounts receivable system. Each of these ten organizations had well-managed and tightly controlled accounts receivable. She was let go.

6. Determine whether the leader holds himself or herself accountable for the performance of an operation. The most senior leader is ultimately responsible for the performance of an operation. This means that every CEO is responsible for the performance of the entire organization as well as its suboperations. While she holds ultimate accountability, she delegates some of that responsibility and accountability to her chiefs, who in turn delegate to presidents, vice presidents, directors, and so on down the line to individual workers. This multidimensional accountability matrix between leader and subordinate makes several people accountable for the same operation. All have some accountability.

However, time and again, when poor performance is brought to light during a performance improvement project, I have witnessed an executive excuse himself or herself and place the blame on a subordinate vice president or director. Even when the poor performance has gone on for years, the executive will not take any accountability. To save face, they terminate a vice president or director. In these cases, the senior executive should have taken control of the poorly performing department when it first started going downhill, rather than letting it go indefinitely and then finally blaming and firing a subordinate.

If a vice president has allowed a director, for instance, to produce substandard results over an extended period of time, the vice president is more accountable for the poor results than the director because they have ultimate stewardship over the operation. Leaders who bear this responsibility are exemplary because they don't allow poor performance to continue at any operational level. I remember listening to a Division One college football postgame show on the radio. After the game was over, the team's new head coach told the listening audience that he was responsible for the loss that day. He could have blamed his assistant coaches, players, referees, injuries, and so on, but he put the loss squarely on his own shoulders. The next season, that coach won his conference and bowl game.

Usually, the fastest way to improve the performance of an underperforming operation is to appoint the right leader. Once in place, she will recruit competent managers and staff, implement optimal key performance targets, set and manage appropriate budgets, and implement proper systems and processes to make operations soar.

Leadership Compensation

Once leadership has been assessed, it is critical to establish appropriate management compensation. Inflated salaries hurt the bottom line and, ironically, can produce complacent managers, while inferior compensation can be demoralizing and also negatively affect productivity. Lowering base pay while increasing bonus and incentive structures can be an effective way to motivate leaders. Typical bonus structures are based on a percentage of a leader's income. For instance, it is common practice for managers to receive 10 percent of their compensation in bonuses, directors twenty percent, vice presidents twenty-five percent, and presidents and executives thirty percent or more. Although these percentages may or may not be ideal, the key is to lower base salaries enough so leaders are continually driven by bonus and incentive plans that ensure consistent performance at optimal levels. Individual bonus plans seem to induce more motivation for higher performance than do companywide or departmentwide bonus plans. Group bonuses, while appropriate in some cases, can dilute individual accountability and performance. A good balance between the two may be optimal.

Leadership salary levels should be vigilantly monitored to make sure they are commensurate with actual performance and not unnecessarily high or low. It is wise for Human Resources to regularly conduct market salary reviews to ensure that leadership salaries are appropriate. Some leaders are paid outrageously high salaries but do not provide the organization with appropriate returns on investment for their work.

In addition, merit must precede and justify pay increases, and never the reverse. I remember once giving in to a manager who had pestered me for a salary raise for some time. I finally caved, thinking that a salary raise would provide the necessary incentive for him to work harder and be more productive. I was wrong; his performance remained the same. In retrospect, I should have demanded his incremental value before I gave him the raise.

TASK 4

ANALYZE FRONTLINE EMPLOYEE PRODUCTIVITY, STAFFING, AND COMPENSATION

After you have assessed the organizational structure and leadership, the next task is to analyze frontline employee productivity, staffing, and compensation. Significant operational opportunities can be realized when frontline staff are productive, when the right staff are in the right positions, and when staff are properly compensated.

➤ **Productivity.** The first step in this task is to examine the productivity of frontline staff. Assuming that frontline staff are well-trained, skilled employees, productivity encompasses both the quantity and quality of an employee's work. It also includes employees performing according to certain behavioral standards set by the organization. In addition, productivity occurs when employees' work is aligned to the performance targets of the operation for which they were hired and also to the business objectives of the organization.

Making an assessment of the quantity and quality of work performed by frontline employees helps determine the right number of employees to staff. It also shows whether the right employees have been hired and whether they are high performers or low performers who need to be managed up or out of the organization.

When assessing the quantity of work, the amount of work performed is usually based upon a particular time period such as hours, days, weeks, pay periods, and months, as well as a "volume driver" or "work load driver" such as volume or throughput. Once these metrics have been identified, the quantity of work can be easily calculated and monitored.

Next, you need to incorporate quality targets to ensure that work is performed in an accurate, complete, qualitative, and timely manner. Without measuring quality standards, employees may produce high quantities of work but allow quality to suffer. Likewise, if quality is overemphasized, the quantity of work may suffer. Therefore, it is critical that operational performance targets are developed for both the quantity and quality of work. They can be developed from industry benchmarks, internal historical data, time and motion studies, and so forth.

Once these performance metrics and targets are in place, you can manage employees based on their outcomes. In this respect, employees don't need to be managed much in terms of process, which gives them more latitude to guide their own work. Managing by outcomes allows high- and low-performing employees to be easily identified. High-performing employees must be retained, while underperforming employees must be managed up to achieve higher levels of performance, or they must be managed out of the organization.

As a new associate administrator for a particular organization, I established productivity targets for my department, which consisted of 500 employees. After analyzing the productivity of each employee, I determined that fifty employees, or ten percent, were significantly underperforming. I then calculated that if half of these fifty employees increased their productivity to targeted performance, I could let the other twenty-five employees go and save money in labor costs. Through attrition, this is precisely what happened. As twenty-five of these fifty employees left, I did not hire replacements, since the remaining employees achieved their performance targets.

In this era of extreme competition, not only do we have to watch productivity and labor costs, we have to recruit employees who possess ideal behavioral standards. High performers are no longer evaluated on just the quantity and quality of their work but also on their honesty, attitude, customer service, friendliness, reliability, respect, and so forth. These traits aren't easily quantifiable, although they indirectly impact operational outcomes through improved customer relations, culture, employee retention, conscientiousness to costs and details, etc.

When an operation is staffed by employees with negative behavioral qualities, it is sometimes necessary to formalize behavioral expectations in a document. I've seen managers outline their expected behavioral expectations, and then, commit their employees to them in writing so they can be held accountable. Otherwise, some employees can be challenging if they think certain behaviors are permissible.

Below are a few behavioral standards required of high-performing staff:

- Demonstrates a positive attitude and pleasant demeanor and is responsive to others.

- Maintains the highest level of service and respect toward customers, vendors, and coworkers.

- Is not critical, demeaning, vindictive, or distracting to coworkers.

- Is open to feedback from coworkers, managers, and vendors.

- Fosters a collaborative work environment through frequent, open communications and teamwork.

- Is completely honest and has integrity.

- Is self-motivated, self-managed, highly productive, and professional.

- Proactively supports the organization's and department-level goals, directions, and aspirations and aligns work accordingly.

- Proactively contributes to making the organization efficient and cost effective.

➤ **Staffing.** Using the quantity and quality performance targets developed above, a manager can then determine how to right-size the staffing and ensure that the right employees are in the right positions. For instance, if a warehouse needed to fill 1,000 customer orders a day and the employee performance target was to pull fifty orders a day with no errors, the warehouse manager needs twenty employees. Very simple math.

However, some departments are more complicated to staff because they require more metrics, such as a customer call center. In this case, a manager may need to look at additional metrics, such as customer satisfaction, first call resolution, abandonment rate, handle time, hold time, and others, to determine the right staffing model.

The best staffing models also incorporate volume fluctuations, which can make staffing more complicated. The healthcare industry has this fairly well dialed in as they use part-time, per-diem, float pools, contract labor, and on-call staff to flex up and flex down when patient volumes increase and decrease. In addition, organizations usually supplement employee pay with overtime, holiday, on-call, and shift differential pay for those working inconvenient times to cover shift needs.

➤ **Compensation.** Once high-performing frontline staff are in place, as well as proper staffing models, the next step is to review employee compensation. Employee compensation includes salaries, wages, benefits, overtime and shift differential pay, bonuses, incentives, and commissions. Benchmark information by geographic region and job position is often available by industry, which can help determine appropriate compensation. Because labor costs can be such a significant portion of an organization's total costs, they must be well managed for an operation to perform profitably. Conversely, inferior compensation can make it challenging to recruit and retain high performing staff.

When looking at staffing and compensation, most managers prefer to staff their areas with fewer, higher-performing employees, who cost a little more, than to staff them with a larger number of mediocre, lower-paid employees. Unfortunately, human resources and administration will often force salary caps when recruiting certain positions, rather than making adjustments for ideal candidates who cost more but do more work.

As a result, better candidates turn down salary offers, and mediocre employees are hired in their place. This can be pennywise and pound foolish. When it comes to hiring, the proverb: "You get what you pay for" usually applies. High-quality staff and managers offset their increased compensation through higher productivity and better operational outcomes. These staff work faster and better. They manage costs more carefully. They reduce employee turnover. They offer new product and operational efficiency ideas. And they enhance revenue by improving customer loyalty. Surprisingly, an astounding number of organizations continue to employ higher numbers of mediocre employees.

On the other hand, some organizations overpay their staff and don't hold them accountable for performance. Employees who find themselves in this situation often become complacent and feel entitled to higher pay and lower performance. The key is to offer the appropriate compensation in order to attract, recruit, and retain the right number of high-performing employees. Once these higher-performing employees are in place, they keep the pressure and accountability on themselves to perform at higher levels and often don't even need to be managed.

TASK 5

UNDERSTAND AND FLOWCHART PROCESSES

The next operational review step is to understand and flowchart the processes of an underperforming operation. This is a vitally important step where the details of every task are carefully documented and analyzed. While this step largely focuses on the tangible, non-human components of the operation, the intangible, human components are also observed. The purpose of flowcharting processes is to identify and visually map out where fragmentation, redundancies, inefficiencies, bottlenecks, breakdowns, and manual processes occur so they can be redesigned, streamlined, automated, and economized. As processes are flowcharted in detail, the goal is to minimize the associated non-value-added steps while optimizing operational outcomes such as quality, quantity, cost, and speed.

Sometimes processes are so enormous and complex that they must be visually flowcharted just to be comprehended. Flowcharting a process begins with the inputs of an operation and ends with the outputs. Once again, the most effective way to flowchart a process is to jump into the operation yourself in order to really understand it. By doing this, processes can be observed firsthand, while at the same time frontline staff can be interviewed and shadowed to gain a full understanding of the operation. Integrating into the operation also allows a natural interaction with customers, vendors, and other parties, which provides additional information.

Because staff live and breathe the operation every day, they can provide critical information unavailable to managers. Frontline staff may also be able to provide a more accurate understanding of the working culture, leadership, productivity, systems, equipment, tools, facilities, and so on. In addition, frontline staff can help pinpoint problems and opportunities, uncover the causes of the problems, and even provide potential solutions. Because staff may have worked on the same process for many years or may have come from other companies in the same industries, they often have unique insights and are just waiting for the opportunity to share them.

Asking an employee about specific work tasks or how processes flow are good conversation openers that can lead to other, perhaps even more important information about the operation. Sometimes, however, employees feel uncomfortable, even vulnerable and threatened, when asked about the details of their work, how various processes function and flow, and other information about an operation. Therefore, be sure to first get approval and backing from direct line managers before talking to employees. Ask managers to inform staff that you will be shadowing them and looking for ways to do things better. Even under these conditions, it is nearly impossible to eliminate all the anxiety people may feel during an operational review, as they are concerned about potential changes and how they will be personally affected. They may also be worried that the interviewer will report something they have done wrong.

High performers usually welcome an operational review and are supportive, while low performers can be closed and resent your presence. In my experience, about half the employees of an underperforming operation are initially open and helpful, while the other half are apprehensive and closed. Some, in fact, may be so open and honest that they won't hide anything—even if it affects their own jobs. I recall an instance when a nurse told me we needed to eliminate her position along with three other highly paid nurses who were doing clerical work.

minute, not only surprising the patient but also the floor nurses, case managers, and social workers. Patients were suddenly asked to contact family members or friends for rides home. However, family and friends were often at work or in the middle of something important, which delayed a ride home. I also learned that many nurses were overworked and reluctant to discharge their healthier patients, who were ready to go home. This was because as soon as a nurse discharged a patient who was ready to go home, they immediately got another, sicker patient who needed more care. This added to the nurse's heavy load.

Finally, the truth of the situation came out as I built trust with the nursing staff and physicians. I recall one patient who was so eager to go home that he had made his bed, gotten dressed, and was sitting on his bed waiting hour after hour for his physician to write his discharge orders. I paged his physician to ask why he hadn't written the discharge order yet. He was in the middle of surgery when he called me back and told me he had been in the operating room since 3:00 a.m. that morning, taking care of several emergency cases. The last thing on his mind was writing the discharge order for a healthy patient who was ready to go home. In essence, the truth of the problem was far more complex than the information received during the interview process.

During this discovery phase of flowcharting processes, when u think you have discovered a significant finding, it's easy to get ited, and you may be tempted to immediately publicize your ing. Don't do it! Show the discipline of waiting until the entire tional review is complete and your findings have been con- . Novice consultants get themselves into trouble when they ey have stumbled onto a major opportunity and immediately yone what they found. In fact, I have watched consultants

Over time, as you build trust with employees, most will begin to appreciate your help and presence as they realize their jobs will become more meaningful, efficient, and productive. Another way to build trust is to always give employees recognition and credit for the information and potential solutions they provide. Improving a process is a collaborative effort, so it is important not to take credit for others' input.

When flowcharting processes, many consultants only interview managers and higher-level leaders to obtain the information they need. Unfortunately, these consultants don't realize until later that their flowcharts are usually laden with mistakes and that they missed vital intricacies. Interviews can provide an informative overview of an operation, but deeper information comes from seeing and feeling the process firsthand until you completely understand it.

While flowcharting a particular hospital's patient flow processes, nursing management informed me that bottlenecks occurred when patients were waiting for a ride home, causing new patients to wait before getting a bed. Based on this feedback, they recommende that a discharge lounge, where patients could wait for their ri be built. They also wanted to modify two hospital vans in or transport patients in wheelchairs and beds to their homes these recommendations were implemented, I put on scru firm that these bottlenecks were accurate. After being o and unit in the hospital for some time and observing th processes in detail, I discovered the actual root cau flow bottlenecks.

While on the surface it appeared that pati rides, I discovered the real reason patients we physicians were not notifying patients in ad be discharged. Physicians regularly wrot inform others that they just found a multimillion-dollar opportunity, only to later discover they were wrong. Once the word is out and the CEO has heard the news and passed it on to the administrative team and board members, you're in a real pickle. Interestingly, CEOs never forget good news. So, if you are wrong, it's very difficult to regain credibility after disclosing a mistake in your findings.

Unfortunately, this is where so many improvement projects go wrong. Information is taken at face value without verifying or confirming the truth. Consequently, poor recommendations are made and implemented that don't correct the real problems. I have learned to be skeptical about the information I receive until it is confirmed during a thorough process review. A consulting boss of mine once told me years ago, "We are paid skeptics."

TASK 6

REVIEW THE PHYSICAL ASSETS, LAYOUT, AND LOCATIONS OF THE PROCESS

While Task 5 reviews the process or function of an operation, its successor, Task 6, reviews the form. This parallels the axiom "form follows function," meaning that the right physical components and structure must be built to optimally facilitate the process and not the other way around. Therefore, after processes have been flowcharted, the next logical task is to review the physical assets of the operation (i.e., the systems, equipment, facilities, tools, vehicles, etc.), as well as the physical layout and various geographical locations that make up the process.

➢ **Physical Assets.** When reviewing the physical assets of an operation, each item should be assessed in terms of its capacity, proficiency, speed, cost, productivity, and reliability in order to evaluate its value to the process and the outcomes it produces. Bottlenecks, high maintenance and repair costs, quality problems, and volume limitations must be identified so solutions can be recommended. Ask these three basic questions when assessing physical assets:

1. Is the asset underperforming? Physical assets that hinder operations from delivering desirable outcomes may need to be improved, repaired, upgraded, replaced, or eliminated. For instance, are there computer systems that have not been upgraded or that are experiencing interface problems with other systems? Is a facility dilapidated and

providing unacceptable and unsafe working conditions? Is office space too small to adequately handle the necessary work volume? Are older generations of equipment being used that negatively affect productivity and operational outcomes? Inadequate physical assets not only hinder positive operational outcomes; they also adversely affect the morale of employees who use the substandard tools and facilities. This in turn exacerbates poor outcomes.

2. Is the asset underutilized? Idle assets are a waste of resources and need to be utilized, taken offline, or sold. Imagine the underutilization of an airplane that just sits in a hangar, a crane that is seldom used to erect buildings, a manufacturing plant that operates only three days a week, a large warehouse storing few inventory items, office suites with few employees, parked trucks not making deliveries, or unused acres of good commercial land. Something must be done with these idle resources to eliminate costs or enhance revenue.

    However, it is vital to never force the use of an underutilized item just because it was already purchased and represents a sunk cost. For instance, when I first began consulting hospital emergency departments, I saw time and again the underutilization of "Computers On Wheels" or "COWs," as the staff called them. These devices were wireless computers connected to the hospital's patient information system and mounted on a stand with wheels. The idea was to push them from room to room for patient registrations. However, as a consultant, I saw COWs at hospital after hospital, sitting in corners and collecting dust.

The registration staff thought they were too cumbersome to move in and out of rooms, so the staff instead used clipboards and paper to collect patient information that was entered into a computer after a registrar returned to their desk. It was a more efficient process than using COWs. At one hospital, administration forced the registration staff to use the COWs just because the computers had been purchased. The staff resented the mandate, as the COWS were inefficient and the wireless connection often failed.

3. Is the asset too costly? A cost-benefit analysis will reveal that some physical assets are simply too expensive to operate, maintain, or upgrade when compared to the benefit they provide. Alternatives should always be considered. For example, a downtown office in a major city may be more expensive than an equally practical office in a suburb, or luxurious vehicles may be too expensive for making client deliveries. Although vendor contracts can sometimes be renegotiated to lower equipment, lease, and maintenance costs, it is sometimes best to find less costly, more practical alternatives.

➤ **Layout and Locations.** The primary purpose of reviewing the physical layout and geographic locations of an operation is to ensure that the process is most effective in terms of maximizing efficiency, economy, revenue, competitive positioning, and so on. To determine this, assess the operation's current layout based on:

- Proximity to preceding and succeeding operations

- Proximity to suppliers and customers

- Locations of competitors

- Weather conditions, transportation, and communication media

- General operating costs of the geographic area

- Cost and standard of living for employees

- Available labor market to support the organization

- Political factors, tax rates, governmental regulations

To complete a layout and location assessment, it is wise to start with a pictorial layout of the current operation, mapping all locations, physical facilities, and major capital assets. Once this illustration is complete, each location and physical component can be separately evaluated on how they contribute to or impede operational outcomes. For example:

- A distribution operation may include warehouses across the nation or globe. Each warehouse location must be reviewed to ensure it is ideal from a cost, customer, supplier, and regulatory perspective, as well as many other factors.

- A large steel manufacturing plant may consist of many different facilities spread over numerous acres of land. These facilities must be reviewed to determine if their proximity to each other is ideal while considering the best means of transporting steel from facility to facility.

- A medical practice established in a particular state may receive less revenue for surgeries than if it were located in a different state where reimbursement rates are higher.

- An office layout should be set up so related functional areas are adjacent in order to perpetuate efficient communications and information flow.

Once the layout and location problems and opportunities are specifically identified, solutions can be proposed and modeled to see how the outcomes can improve.

TASK 7

EXAMINE THE INPUTS

The next step to assessing the current state of an operation is to examine the inputs. Sometimes, inputs can be improved faster, with a much larger financial and quality impact on an operation than redesigning processes or changing the physical assets, location, and layout.

Inputs are information, ideas, supplies, money, and even people that are transformed, modified, converted, or altered in some manner during an operation to produce intended outcomes, outputs, or deliverables. If an element of an input is defective or problematic, it can obviously affect the final deliverable. For instance, inaccurate financial information generates inaccurate month-end accounting reports; bad customer information results in incorrect billing and collections; high fuel costs result in high shipping costs, supply distribution delays cause product delays; flawed bricks make flawed homes; and bad ad copy produces bad advertisements.

In regards to inputs, especially faulty information or defective supplies, the adage "garbage in equals garbage out" holds true. While working for a large manufacturing facility, I was asked to review a newly installed computerized order-entry manufacturing system to determine why it was suddenly causing a surge in manufacturing errors and customer returns. After reviewing the system, I found that the manufacturing errors were not caused by this costly system but by the way customer orders were entered into the system. Customer orders were entered by a group of thirty-five clerks, none of whom were held accountable for accurately entering information. This group was more concerned about the quantity of orders than the quality.

Inaccurate order entry caused manufacturing to produce the wrong items, which were then shipped to customers, resulting in customer returns. The solution was quick, simple, and inexpensive—hold the clerks accountable for accuracy. This was accomplished by first comparing production errors, which were identified from customer returns, to the original customer order sheets to determine what errors were made. Next, the clerks who made the errors were easily identified, as the system kept track of which clerks entered each order. The clerks were individually held accountable for their mistakes. Consistent errors could ultimately cost a clerk his job. Production quality, needless to say, was immediately restored.

Frontend and Backend Quality Control

Ideally, quality control procedures and safeguards should be placed at the beginning and end of an operation. Prior to entering an operation, inputs should be quickly inspected to ensure they meet key quality standards. At the end of an operation, outputs are also inspected to ensure that quality standards are met. Figure 16 illustrates the quality control points at the beginning and end of an operation.

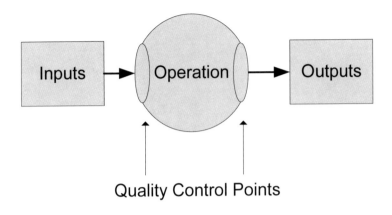

Figure 16: **Quality control points of an operation**

These frontend and backend quality control points should track every important quality indicator, including defects, accuracy, reliability, wait times, and so forth. When quality errors are identified at the beginning of an operation, they should be documented and shared with the preceding operation or the external vendors who provided the inputs, so mistakes can be corrected. In fact, those who oversee the preceding operations (including external vendors) whose outputs are your inputs should supply you with quality reports showing they have inspected their outputs. This will help ensure they have quality controls at the backend of their operations. It may be wise to clearly delineate in vendor contracts the need for these quality reports. When quality errors do slip through the preceding operation, hopefully your frontend quality checks catch the errors before they go into the operations.

Unfortunately, defective inputs can still slip through the cracks. After starting Kodiak Cakes, on occasion, an external production vendor would inadvertently omit a key food ingredient, such as salt. Or they added an incorrect ingredient, such as the wrong kind of whole wheat. So, even though these mistakes passed through their frontend and backend quality control points, we set up additional quality controls to ensure these types of errors didn't make it to the customer.

Before an organization purchases inputs from an external vendor, the vendor organization must be evaluated. This will ensure that prospective vendors are solvent and customer-oriented. Just because a vendor can produce an exceptional product doesn't mean they will support it, deliver it reliably, or be around a few years down the road. Therefore, it should become standard to perform vendor evaluations during the "Request for Proposal" stage and negotiation process before purchasing products and services from a particular vendor.

Input Pricing

As vendors are evaluated to ensure quality, customer service, solvency, and so forth, it is also critical to purchase inputs at the best price, to control operational costs. A few key strategies can be employed for achieving the best pricing.

First, when possible, negotiate vendor pricing based on the use of group purchasing organizations (GPOs) and benchmark information. Group purchasing organizations are made up of many member organizations that pool their buying power to negotiate deep volume discounts with vendors. Benchmark information, on the other hand, simply tells an organization what other organizations in the same industry and geographical region are currently paying for specific items from specific vendors. When reviewing benchmark information, you may find that you are paying an excessive price for certain materials and supplies in comparison to what others are paying. This information can be used to negotiate better pricing.

Next, once the best price has been negotiated, the agreed-upon price should always be written up in a pricing agreement or vendor contract. This will avoid pricing disagreements in the future. It is critical that a purchasing agreement or vendor contract be in place for every item an organization purchases from every vendor. This ensures that some sort of negotiation has taken place between the organization and each vendor. Otherwise, vendors may be charging list price—their highest price. This is like going to a car dealership and paying the list or sticker price without attempting to negotiate. Most vendors, like car dealerships, will reduce their initial pricing.

As a rule, vendor contracts should typically not exceed three years so that if superior technology and supplies are developed in the future, the purchasing organization is not locked into a long-term agreement. The exercise of making sure pricing for all items an organization purchases has been negotiated and is in a contract is referred to as "contract negotiations." Once a contract is in place, it is critical to ensure that the price charged by the vendor on an invoice actually meets the price stipulated in the contract. It is common to find invoice errors in which vendors inadvertently charge higher prices than agreed upon. Ensuring parity between prices charged on a vendor invoice and prices stated on a vendor contract is referred to as "contract compliance."

Often, organizations will conduct a three-way pricing match. This is where they compare the contracted price to the purchase order price and then to the invoice. Purchase order spend reports, broken down by item, can be compared to vendor invoice spend reports, also broken down by item, over a period of time. This way, you can uncover pricing discrepancies over time. Vendor billing mistakes can cost organizations millions of dollars.

Finally, vendor contracts that are about to expire must be renegotiated and re-contracted in advance—an exercise known as "contract management." This is necessary because when contracts expire, vendors will often immediately raise their pricing back to list prices.

Unless these rate changes are caught by the purchasing organization, the higher prices will ultimately affect the profitability of the operation. In addition, contracts should contain a clause stating that once the contract expires, the contracted pricing remains in effect until a new contract is established. This puts the onus back on the vendor to begin the renegotiating process, rather than allowing them to automatically revert to list pricing.

To get to the best possible contract price, the purchasing organization should also look for opportunities to consolidate and standardize the items they buy. This allows the organization to purchase a single item in larger quantities and receive volume discounts from one vendor, rather than purchasing multiple items from multiple vendors at higher prices. For instance, some hospitals purchase many different kinds of medical/surgical gloves from various vendors. However, significant money can be saved with volume discounts resulting from standardizing the purchase of gloves—that is, purchasing just one type or fewer types of gloves.

In addition, standardizing inputs can generate efficiencies that reduce the number of inventory items, processes, machinery, and procedures to manage. This is why some restaurants sell fewer menu items. It allows them not only to standardize the ingredients but also to consolidate the processes required to prepare different entrées. Some Mexican restaurants use virtually the same process to make several related dishes using the same beans, rice, tortillas, cheese, lettuce, and tomatoes. In many cases, only the sauces and meats vary, or how the dish is arranged.

A final way to leverage pricing is to explore and identify alternative items or inputs that are less costly but perform at the same or better levels. Less expensive generic products, for example, can often perform at the same levels as expensive name-brand products.

Usage and Inventory Management

After essential inputs are purchased at the optimal price, they must be used and managed judiciously. The proper use of inputs helps prevent waste and overuse that otherwise would unnecessarily escalate costs. As a hospital operations consultant, I observed that operating rooms routinely incur excessive costs as unused supplies and instruments are discarded. I also witnessed extremely expensive chemotherapy drugs disposed of when patients failed to show up for their appointments. In addition, some emergency room physicians were using more expensive antibiotics when less expensive ones were sufficient. When operations are altered so inputs are used more efficiently, the costs of the operations and ultimately the outcomes are reduced, while profits rise.

In addition, when inputs become inventory for an operation, they must be managed carefully to ensure products aren't damaged, stolen, wasted, or spoiled. Moreover, inventory levels (commonly referred to as "par levels") must not be too low or too high. While consulting hospitals, I routinely saw the over-purchasing of items, such as expensive bottles of unused lab reagents that had to be discarded after their six-month shelf life had expired.

Deficient inventories cause operational delays and bottlenecks while an operation waits for inputs to arrive. On the other hand, excessive inventories can result in cash flow problems as inaccessible funds are tied up. High inventory levels can also generate high carrying costs, such as storage, maintenance, and security costs. Furthermore, internal inventory distribution must be carried out efficiently and economically through smart logistics and effective means of transportation.

TASK 8

REVIEW PURCHASED SERVICES

Organizations frequently outsource many services within an operation, if not the entire operation itself, to outside vendors. Manufacturing, sales, information technology, marketing, legal, accounting, construction, billing, collections, human resources, valet parking, architecture, tax preparation, landscaping, janitorial services, customer service, and repairs and maintenance are just a few examples of the countless services that can be outsourced. Each is an operation, or a function within an operation. When I started Kodiak Cakes, a food manufacturing company, I initially outsourced the legal, graphic design, production, purchasing, distribution, and sales functions.

When an operation or function is outsourced, you no longer have full control over it. The purpose of reviewing purchased services is similar to reviewing the inputs of an operation—to assess the services rendered in terms of their cost, quality, timeliness, quantity, and other performance standards. These service outcomes should then be compared against the performance expectations agreed upon. It is wise to ensure that all vendor agreements are contractually written so that performance standards and expectations are clearly specified. Vendor contracts should also stipulate that the vendor assumes responsibility for monitoring and reporting key performance indicators for the services they provide. These key performance indicators will show whether the vendor is meeting operational expectations. Leaders can then discuss with vendors any negative variances between actual and expected outcomes to determine where and why problems are occurring.

When I first outsourced the production of Kodiak Cakes, we experienced problems with several vendors. One vendor had significant quality problems. A second vendor could not handle the volumes. A third vendor went out of business. A fourth vendor's pricing escalated to the point that it was too costly to continue doing business with them. Finally, we settled on a fifth vendor, whose outcomes met expectations on a continuous basis.

When purchased services are critical to the outcomes of an internal operation, it is prudent to have a secondary or backup vendor in place. In fact, it is not only good to have secondary vendors on deck for purchased services but also for supply vendors who provide operational inputs. When a primary vendor fails to deliver, an operation can temporarily shut down. Consequently, succeeding operations are suspended, and myriad problems begin to arise. Costs escalate, orders aren't filled, customer relations are damaged, and sales decrease.

Some organizations will use two or three primary vendors concurrently in order to foster high performance through competition. It is common practice for organizations to outsource old and unpaid accounts receivable to three different collection agencies. An organization simply splits up their accounts receivable list in three ways, sending uncollected accounts to the three different vendors. Performance is then tracked for each vendor to determine who has the highest collection rates and lowest costs. This way, the organization can continually compare the pricing and performance of each vendor.

For complex organizations that contract with hundreds of vendors, the method for assessing costs and services associated with purchased services must be performed in a systematic way. The best way to perform a department- or even an organization-wide vendor review is to obtain a twelve-month vendor spend report from the organization's accounts payable department. This report lists all vendors with whom a department or the organization as a whole has done business. The summary should then be sorted in descending order of total spend so that vendors who were paid the most are at the top of the list.

Once the vendor spend summary report is generated, the first task is to ensure that a current vendor contract exists for services performed by each vendor. The contract should be reviewed to ensure specific performance criteria such as cost, quality, delivery, customer service, performance monitoring, and other provisions are listed. Second, the vendor's services should be evaluated in terms of how their performance met their contractual obligations. Third, the vendor costs should then be assessed to determine whether pricing renegotiation opportunities exist. Benchmark information may exist from associations, benchmarking companies, or group purchasing organizations to assist with renegotiations. Fourth, the organization should determine whether alternative means exist to reduce costs. For instance, can the services of two or more vendors be consolidated into just one vendor to obtain volume discounts? Can the services be done in-house at a lower cost? Can the services be used less frequently? Should a request for a a proposal be issued to generate competitive bids? Once you evaluate these four areas (contract, outcomes, pricing, and alternatives), the decision can be made to renew a contract, terminate a contract, or solicit bids.

Findings Report

As mentioned earlier, as each of the eight operational review tasks is completed, it is important to summarize the key problems and opportunities identified in *Findings Report*. While this report should be brief and succinct, it must be very specific. Findings reports that make statements such as "processes are fragmented," "the working culture is lax," "management does not hold staff accountable," "manual processes exist," and "staff show no ownership" are not helpful. Findings reports need to specify the exact systems, people, processes, equipment, facilities, and so forth to isolate the problems, causes, and impacts on efficiency, quality, and outcomes. In addition, wherever possible, each of the problems or opportunities listed in the *Findings Report* should be supported with data. Data provides the empirical evidence that quantifies a problem or an opportunity and makes it a believable fact.

I have read numerous findings reports produced by expensive consulting firms. Far too many are written in general terms, providing less useful information. The goal of a *Findings Report* is to list the specific problems, measurable opportunities, causes, and supportive data so solutions and recommendations can be developed to address them. As a reminder, during each of the eight operational review tasks discussed in this chapter, potential solutions should have been identified along the way. These potential solutions should be documented so they can be referenced during Step 5, Recommend Operational Improvements.

CHAPTER SUMMARY: Key Points

1. Step 3 to optimizing performance is to evaluate underperforming operations in order to understand and identify specific problems and opportunities for improvement. Approximately twenty-five percent of a performance improvement project is devoted to this step.

2. When several underperforming operations have been identified in Stage 1, Opportunity Analysis, operations showing the most urgent need and greatest financial opportunity should be evaluated first.

3. Evaluating an underperforming operation consists of getting to the truth or the root cause of problems so correct recommendations can be made.

4. During the operational review, begin looking for possible solutions. In particular, ask leaders and staff what they would do differently to optimize operations.

5. There are eight sequential tasks to accomplish when reviewing an operation.

   Task 1: Determine whether the operation should exist.

   Task 2: Review the organizational structure by examining the following six components:
   1) Functional alignment
   2) Management levels
   3) Spans of control
   4) Job titles

5) Cost centers and budgets

6) Physical layout

Task 3: Evaluate leadership and their compensation. When assessing leadership, review the following six items:

1) Evaluate the outcomes and deliverables of the operation that the leader oversees.

2) Evaluate the trends of the outcomes to see if they generally improve or decline.

3) Assess the culture.

4) Observe how the leader responds to the scrutiny of his or her operation.

5) Observe whether the leader blames the systems, facilities, equipment, tools, and inputs for poor outcomes.

6) Determine whether the leader holds himself accountable for the performance of the operation.

Task 4: Analyze frontline productivity, staffing, and compensation.

Task 5: Understand and flowchart processes.

Task 6: Review the physical assets, layout, and location of the process. Regarding physical assets, evaluate the following:

- Is the asset underperforming?

- Is the asset underutilized?

- Is the asset too costly?

Task 7: Examine the inputs, by examining the following:

- Frontend and backend quality control points

- Input pricing

- Usage and inventory management

Task 8: Review purchased services.

6. Once each task is complete, a *Findings Report* is written. It succinctly summarizes specific problems and opportunities for improvement, so precise recommendations can be made to address them.

7. Potential solutions discovered during the eight operational review tasks are documented so they can be referenced during Step 5, Recommend Operational Improvements.

STEP 4

Benchmark Best Practice Organizations

PHASE I. ASSESSMENT
Stage I - Opportunity Analysis
Step 1: Measure current performance
Step 2: Establish performance targets
Stage II - Operational Review
Step 3: Evaluate underperforming operations
Step 4: Benchmark best practice organizations
PHASE II. IMPLEMENTATION
Stage III - Recommendations & implementation
Step 5: Recommend operational improvements
Step 6: Implement recommendations
Stage IV - Sustainability & Refinement
Step 7: Monitor outcomes
Step 8: Refine improvements

Step 4 to optimizing performance is benchmarking best-practice organizations to help determine solutions to the operational problems and opportunities identified in Step 3. You should devote approximately 10 percent of your performance improvement project to this step. Once you have completed Step 3 and identified an operation's problems and opportunities, the underlying causes, as well as potential solutions, it is time to explore further potential solutions in greater depth. The basis for Step 4 is the *Findings Report*, developed in Step 3.

After a performance improvement team has reviewed the *Findings Report*, some solutions will be readily identified. However, during Step 4, you will identify additional solutions through researching other organizations, particularly for the more complex problems and opportunities. Many operational leaders are unwilling to commit the time and effort required by this step. However, one way to avoid failure is to discover and implement solutions that have proven successful at other organizations. Step 4 is an important stepping stone to finalizing the best recommendations for Step 5, Recommend Operational Improvements.

Step 4 requires asking other organizations to share their experience with similar operational challenges you are facing so you can learn from them. Many individuals feel uncomfortable contacting other organizations, finding the right people to talk to, and asking them for their insight and feedback on operational issues. Conducting such research will prevent you from wasting valuable time and resources while attempting to implement costly recommendations. Don't reinvent the wheel!

In addition, benchmarking not only helps organizations identify the correct solutions but also accelerates the implementation process. The information obtained from benchmarking adds credibility and confidence to your recommendations. Senior leadership is more apt to approve, support, and implement such recommendations more quickly because the risks are minimized and the projected returns appear more certain. Your organization may actually be able to further refine what other organizations have done which could yield even greater results.

While working in upper management for a large hospital system, I was challenged with the task of improving the hospital's method for setting and managing budgets. After reviewing the outcomes of our budgeting and financial management process, I discovered the hospital had overspent its projected cost budget by millions of dollars. Further analysis showed that about fifty percent of the large negative budget variance was attributable to setting budgets incorrectly. The other fifty percent of the variance was derived from poor budget management, in which managers were not held accountable to their budgets. As I reviewed our budgeting process in more detail, I identified many problems that needed improvement.

In trying to determine the best solutions to these problems, I benchmarked thirty organizations, in which I interviewed fifteen CFOs from best practice medical centers, ten executives from reputable consulting firms, and five budget managers from other leading hospitals. During my benchmarking research, I asked both specific and general questions about the problems we faced. The open-ended questions allowed those I interviewed to provide additional information that I had not considered.

During each phone interview, I took copious notes and typed them into a lengthy document. I was surprised at the duration of each interview and how generous the financial experts were with their time in trying to help our hospital system develop a better budgeting process. In analyzing their responses, I was able to identify common findings as well as unique insights.

After incorporating the feedback from the interviews with the information I obtained from internal leaders and staff during Step 3, I developed a final set of recommendations. Seven specific points targeted how to set more accurate budgets, while another seven outlined how to manage budgets more tightly and hold managers accountable.

The benchmarking information I obtained was crucial because it provided a list of successfully proven solutions based on the experience of industry veterans. As we implemented these solutions, our budget gap significantly decreased, resulting in a year-end financial performance that more closely resembled our financial projections. Accordingly, the hospital was able to stay on track with its short- and long-term financial goals and strategic plans. These plans included building additional facilities, meeting patient needs, and staying more competitive. The information was so valuable, I later published an article based on what I learned from the thirty interviews.

Credibility

The key to success in the example above was the credibility that came from benchmarking external experts. When senior leadership was provided with a set of recommendations, primarily given by highly reputable organizations and experts, the recommendations were taken seriously. Because best practice organizations had proven the recommendations to be successful, the perceived risk of implementing them was much lower. Consequently, the recommendations were quickly approved and implemented. Furthermore, management viewed the recommendations not simply as a list that I had personally created but as a proven list provided by industry authorities. This was a deliberate outcome.

To clarify, one of the goals of benchmarking is to present recommendations in such a way that senior leadership will overlook the consultant or task team and concentrate on the benchmarking sources. The focus of recommendations should be on what other top organizations have done, not on what a consultant or performance improvement team simply proposes. This credibility arms senior leadership with a perceived guarantee of success, which they need in order to approve a set of recommendations that could be costly to implement.

Primary Research

Performing operational benchmarking is quite different from obtaining benchmarks on financial ratios, staffing baselines, vendor pricing comparisons, and other quantitative performance metrics. Operational benchmarking investigates how other organizations actually perform an operation. This type of benchmarking gets to the heart of the tangible and intangible aspects of an operation and includes reviewing equipment, facilities, computer systems, processes, organizational charts, management styles, culture, working environment, employee incentives, operational inputs, policies, and so on. This kind of benchmarking is invaluable because it digs deep, delving beyond the quantitative information that appears on a benchmarking report full of data. It tells an organization how to change and what to change.

Thorough benchmarking can be performed in two ways: primary and secondary research. While secondary research is carried out through literature reviews (that is, reading publications about what others have done), primary research consists of firsthand observation and interaction with people from other organizations. Both types of research can be vital, while one is sometimes more helpful than the other depending on the situation. However, from my experience, primary research usually provides the most valuable information. This is because talking to a real person over the phone, meeting with a group of experts face-to-face, or visiting an actual organization to see it in action firsthand is more comprehensive and meaningful to the senses. Also, since primary benchmark information can be tailored to your specific needs, it can often provide more insightful information than can be communicated in articles and books.

Consider the difference between reading about how to fly an airplane and being in the cockpit next to the pilot, flying through turbulence, observing the instruments, feeling the movement of the plane, and listening to the pilot instruct you through the process. Imagine reading about the manufacturing processes of a huge steel mill versus physically entering the production plant and observing firsthand the stadium-sized factories that house massive pieces of powerful machinery, feeling the heat of the fiery molten ore, and sensing the danger of the black, threatening environment with cranes overhead, trains running behind you, and large scooping buckets the size of small swimming pools. Real-life experiences are immensely different from reading about them because you experience the actual environment, hear the intonations and background noise, and observe expressions and body language. The senses are convincing and communicate the deep core of an organization.

As a hospital operations consultant, I was frequently involved with Emergency Room improvement projects. In order to really learn and understand the Emergency Room and what best practice hospitals were doing, I visited a large number of best practice hospital emergency departments across the United States. It wasn't until I watched inner city emergency rooms full of patients waiting to be seen, trauma victims coming in on stretchers, families weeping over lost loved ones, staff scurrying here and there, security officers standing guard, patients waiting for more than a full day to be admitted because no beds were available in the hospital, as well as the down times when all was comparatively quiet, that I realized which operational solutions work and which do not. Only in this authentic environment, with scrubs on, shadowing nurses, interviewing physicians, watching patients, feeling the highs and lows, and observing the computer systems, the physical facility and layout, and the flow of patients in the morning and late into the night did I discover the operational factors of an efficient emergency department that made a difference.

Benchmarking Methodology

The best way to begin the benchmarking process is to first review the *Findings Report*, which lists the problems and opportunities identified in Step 3, Evaluate Underperforming Operations. The problems and opportunities contained in this report should be arranged in the order of the eight operational review tasks, listed below:

Task 1: Determine whether the operation should exist.

Task 2: Review the organizational structure.

Task 3: Evaluate leadership and their compensation.

Task 4: Analyze frontline staffing, productivity, and compensation.

Task 5: Understand and flowchart processes.

Task 6: Review the physical assets, location, and layout of the process.

Task 7: Examine the inputs.

Task 8: Review purchased services.

After reviewing the findings of these eight tasks, the next step is to identify problems and opportunities requiring further research to determine the best solutions. Once you have identified them, select which organizations to benchmark. Best-practice organizations are inherently successful, and therefore usually provide the best answers. However, while an organization may be considered "best-practice," some of its internal operations might not function ideally. Perhaps they are struggling with the same challenges you are.

In fact, like any other organization, a best-practice organization has probably attempted many improvements that failed as well as some that succeeded. Either scenario can provide great learning opportunities for what to do and what not to do. For example, a benchmark organization that may have developed a homegrown computer system that turned out to be a disaster, could steer you toward a better alternative. At the same time, they may have successfully implemented an important piece of equipment that automates processes and reduces expenses.

Although it is most common to benchmark organizations within the same industry, such as a university benchmarking other universities or an airport benchmarking other airports, the benchmarked organization need not always be in the same industry. For example, if an organization aims to improve certain human resource operations, companies from various industries may be able to provide valuable information and feedback. Furthermore, because of the competitive nature of business, benchmarking outside one's geographic region or industry may be necessary. Stanford and Johns Hopkins medical centers may be comfortable benchmarking with one another about operational questions, because they are on two opposite coasts of the United States. On the other hand, two medical centers located in the same vicinity might be less inclined to share information because they are in direct competition with one another.

That said, competitors can provide great benchmark information since they have similar operations. One way to acquire this information is to identify employees who have worked for competitors in the past and who are not under non-disclosure or non-compete agreements. These employees can provide valuable operational information. At a manufacturing company I consulted, we asked employees who had worked at competing companies how they forecasted production volumes. At a large food company in the eastern United States, we asked employees who had worked at competing companies how these companies marketed their brands and compensated their sales teams.

Years ago, while working for a manufacturing organization, I was asked to improve an employee idea and recognition program. Rather than approaching our direct competitors, I contacted the human resources department of best-practice organizations outside our industry. Some of these companies came from manufacturing, technology, and retail. While on the phone interviewing the human resources directors, I mentioned the purpose of my call and what my organization was trying to accomplish. They were most generous about providing feedback from their own employee idea and recognition programs. I was able to share with administration what I learned, and was also able to make the right recommendations.

Once you have identified the organizations you want to benchmark, it is time to pick up the phone, call the organizations, and ask to be connected to the appropriate departments. After you have made contact with the department, simply explain the purpose of your call and ask who would be the best resource to talk to. You may be transferred to an engineer, an accountant, a department director, or an administrator. Although some people will feel uneasy about talking to you, the vast majority will be most helpful.

During phone interviews, it is important to ask both specific and open-ended questions. While specific questions address specific problems, open-ended questions allow the interviewee to discuss other related areas you may not have previously considered. For instance, if you are benchmarking organizations in an attempt to find out which computer system to purchase for an accounting department, you may want to set up a grid or matrix that lists the different companies you are benchmarking across the left column, with specific questions for them to answer across the top row. Some of your questions may deal with system functionality, reporting, capacity, and technical support. As each question is answered, the answers can go into the specific cells of the matrix. This is a good way to organize detailed feedback.

You should also ask general, open-ended questions as well, such as what their opinion of the system is. At this point, they may tell you that their system interfaced poorly with another key internal system, or that the sales representative from the software company was difficult to work with, or that they have recently learned of a superior system offered by another company.

During phone interviews, it will be apparent that some organizations you talk to run much more efficiently than others. After singling out the best-in-class organizations, it may be beneficial to request an onsite visit, as this is where the real learning takes place. An onsite assessment may reveal that their operation is actually fairly average, running below the optimal standard you had presumed. This information is still helpful if it prevents you from implementing material changes that would have failed.

The information and data obtained through benchmarking should be recorded on a *Benchmarking Report* that is a separate document from the *Findings Report*. The *Benchmarking Report* should contain a summary of your key benchmark findings and useful background information. This report is then used in Step 5 to determine the final set of improvement recommendations to be proposed.

Diminishing Returns

It is wise to benchmark as many organizations as it takes to identify the best solutions. Curtailing the benchmarking process too soon can rob you of valuable feedback and answers to your questions. I deliberately benchmark organizations until I feel I have hit the point of diminishing returns, where further research is unproductive and unnecessary. Once this point has been achieved, solutions to operational challenges begin to crystallize, and it is time to formalize the final set of improvement recommendations.

CHAPTER SUMMARY: Key Points

1. Step 4 to optimizing performance is benchmarking best-practice organizations to determine optimal improvement recommendations. Plan on devoting approximately 10 percent of the improvement project to this step.

2. The *Findings Report*, developed in Step 3, provides the basis for Step 4 because it lists the problems and opportunities of an underperforming operation as well as the root causes.

3. Benchmarking is the critical steppingstone to developing the appropriate set of recommendations. It allows you to largely eliminate the risk of a failed implementation.

4. Recommendations based on benchmarking best-practice organizations are highly credible and accelerate the administrative approval process.

5. While benchmarking consists of both primary and secondary research, primary research usually provides the most valuable information because of the direct communication and firsthand observation of other organizations.

6. The methodology for benchmarking is to identify which operational challenges need to be benchmarked from the *Findings Report* created in Step 3, then determine which organizations to benchmark, and finally contact the organizations and interview key people. Both specific and open-ended questions are important. After singling out organizations that employ the best operations, it is often highly beneficial to request an onsite visit.

7. Benchmarked information is recorded in a *Benchmark Report* that is used in Step 5, Recommend Operational Improvements.

8. To make certain the best solutions have been identified, benchmarking should be taken to the point of diminishing returns.

STEP 5

Recommend Operational Improvements

PHASE I. ASSESSMENT
Stage I - Opportunity Analysis
Step 1: Measure current performance
Step 2: Establish performance targets
Stage II - Operational Review
Step 3: Evaluate underperforming operations
Step 4: Benchmark best practice organizations
PHASE II. IMPLEMENTATION
Stage III - Recommendations & implementation
Step 5: Recommend operational improvements
Step 6: Implement recommendations
Stage IV - Sustainability & Refinement
Step 7: Monitor outcomes
Step 8: Refine improvements

S tep 5 is to recommend the right operational improvements. Recommending optimal operational improvements requires about ten percent of the total project time and is based on achieving the performance targets set in Step 2, Establish Performance Targets. In Step 2, the current outcomes of an operation were compared to the targeted outcomes. The difference between these represented operational opportunities. These opportunities were converted into financial opportunities when possible. The objective of Step 5 is to recommend the best improvements that will realize the operational opportunities by achieving the performance targets.

Much of the groundwork for Step 5 was performed during the analysis and research completed in Steps 3 and 4. In Step 3, Evaluate Underperforming Operations, key operational problems and opportunities were discovered and documented in a *Findings Report*. Potential solutions were also identified in Step 3 by front-line staff, managers, vendors, customers, leaders, and other experts during the eight operational review tasks. In Step 4, Benchmark Best Practice Organizations, the insight and experience of best practice organizations were collected and documented in a *Benchmark Report*. Potential solutions were also identified in Step 4.

Step 5 reviews these reports, considers other information and ideas, and then determines the best recommendations to propose that will optimize operational outcomes. If the analysis and research in Steps 3 and 4 were adequately performed, many of the right solutions would be readily apparent, making Step 5 an easier step to complete.

Recommendations Report

After reviewing the reports from Steps 3 and 4, further study, vetting, brainstorming, and interviews may be needed to determine the very best recommendations. A *Recommendations Report* is then prepared in Step 5 that lists the right recommendations. I like to make this step easier by converting the *Findings Report* from Step 3 into the

Recommendations Report. This way, the problems and opportunities listed in the *Findings Report* are followed by the corresponding improvement solutions and recommendations.

The recommendations listed on the *Recommendations Report* should also include supportive information and data to substantiate them. Benchmarking information, showing what other organizations have successfully implemented, should be included in this report. The costs and resources required to implement specific recommendations, along with their projected return on investment, should be included in this report as well. Charts, tables, other supporting information, and documents providing details about your recommendations should be attached to the report as necessary.

Providing a depiction of the current state compared to the proposed state is very useful in supporting a recommendation. For example, if a recommendation is to restructure a department to be more efficient and save costs, include both the current organizational chart and the proposed organizational chart. If a manual process is to be redesigned and automated, provide both the current and proposed flowcharts. If a facility is to be renovated to enhance process efficiency, provide the current and proposed architectural designs.

With sensitive recommendations, such as replacing a director or proposing a reduction in force, I have found it is better to discuss the details behind these recommendations verbally until senior leadership requests further documentation.

In essence, the *Recommendations Report* is a succinct summary of the operational findings and the corresponding improvement recommendations, along with crucial backup information that administration needs for approval and implementation.

Specific Recommendations

As a reminder, recommendations must be written as specifically as possible, as general recommendations are meaningless because they lack a definitive plan for implementation. For instance, listing a recommendation that states "Change the culture of the department to improve staff accountability" is incomplete. A valuable recommendation might state, "Improve the department culture by promoting accountability through (1) rewriting employee job descriptions that include specific performance and behavioral standards, (2) installing a specific system that tracks individual performance, (3) replacing the department director, and (4) restructuring the management layer so that functional areas are aligned under specific managers. In addition, the details behind each of these recommendations should be provided. Specific recommendations provide value because they are implementable and aimed at improving particular outcomes.

"Provide more staff training" is a common recommendation I see. This particularly popular recommendation is frequently used when insufficient work and effort have gone into identifying the real operational problems. I call it the "training recommendation," which is only valid if substantiated with precise details that outline what specific training is needed, which operational problems will be resolved and how, who will provide the training, the cost of the training, the training objectives, the location of the training, and the expected operational and financial outcomes.

Another dubious recommendation I frequently encounter is when capital purchases are proposed, such as new equipment, facilities, and computer systems. Unless these "capital purchase recommendations" are made with specific and convincing supporting data and financial projections, they tend to be scapegoats for the real, underlying operational and managerial problems. Once the supporting justification for making a capital purchase recommendation has been thoroughly researched and explained, it may prove to be the best solution.

In terms of best solutions, one of the very best I see on a *Recommendations Report* is the proposal to return to an operation's old way of doing things—"the way we used to do it." Whether that includes reimplementing an old process, system, incentive plan, or compensation structure, these types of recommendations are usually on target. Unfortunately, countless leaders and consultants arbitrarily transform an operation when the original process was superior. This is so commonplace.

All Things Considered

When making specific recommendations, be sure all relevant factors are considered. Recommendations should be made in light of the organization's financial situation, its competitive environment, the economy, government and industry regulations, the current labor market, and other relevant factors that could impact a successful implementation. It may seem advantageous to propose reducing labor costs, implementing a state-of-the-art facility, exporting products to a foreign country, or developing a new product line. However, will an organization's labor union agreement allow the recommendation to reduce labor costs in the manner proposed? Can current cash flows and the balance sheet bear the financial burden of a new state-of-the-art facility along with other liabilities? How do international trade policies and tariffs affect the profitability of exporting products? How will competitive products coming to market affect a newly proposed product line? Or could new products infringe on any existing competitor patents? To make the most prudent and sound recommendations, these contextual issues must be examined.

Only after you have considered all relevant factors can you make recommendations with complete assurance and confidence that they are the best. There should be no hesitation or feeling that something was missed during the recommendation process. If you feel any uncertainty, withhold the recommendation until your doubt is resolved. Any trace of misgiving usually signifies a lack of obtaining the necessary information to make a final recommendation. If there is an unclear choice between two potential recommendations, you simply need more information because one is almost always better than the other.

Before finalizing your *Recommendations Report*, it is wise to entitle it, "Draft Recommendations" until key leaders, experts, and stakeholders have a chance to review and respond to the recommendations. Seasoned professionals may add valuable insight that will refine and enhance the final recommendations. They may have had an unsuccessful experience with a similar recommendation. Or they may identify other unforeseen internal and external issues that may alter the success of the recommendations. They may, however, agree with and support each recommendation. Only then can your *Recommendations Report* be made final.

Cost-Benefit

As mentioned above, recommendations that have associated implementation costs and projected financial benefits should be supported by a cost-benefit analysis. The goal of such an analysis is to implement recommendations that minimize costs and maximize returns. A simple ROI (Return On Investment) calculation that compares the cost of implementing a recommendation to its projected net benefit is very useful.

For example, suppose a recommendation is to lease a piece of manufacturing equipment that is expected to replace ten full-time workers, for $500,000 a year. The workers' annual salaries are $100,000 each (including benefits), totaling $1,000,000 a year. To calculate the ROI, you simply take the net benefit (the net income or savings from a proposed recommendation) and divide it by the cost of the investment to improve the operation. You can then convert the result to a percentage by multiplying it by 100 and adding a percentage symbol. In this case, you would take $500,000 as the net savings ($1,000,000 annual labor costs - $500,000 annual equipment cost), then divide it by $500,000 (annual equipment cost). This gives you 1. To get a percentage, multiply 1 by 100 and then add a percentage symbol. The ROI would be a hundred percent.

In other cases, completing a cost-benefit analysis may be more complex, especially when your recommendation includes underlying assumptions and future years. In these cases, you would want to build a pro forma financial statement that shows the net income or loss over future years. For example, suppose a hospital wants to purchase a new MRI machine with a useful life of ten years at a cost of $3 million. In order to determine if this is a wise investment, you would build a pro forma financial statement that would include the depreciation of the asset as well as assumptions about patient volumes, revenue, inflation, etc. Your pro forma would also show your break-even point for the purchase.

Still, some pro formas can be more complicated. Consider, for example, the recommendation to build a new hospital. In such a case, revenues, costs, and patient volumes are projected based on underlying assumptions about population growth, the competitive environment, and inflationary factors. In addition, revenues, costs, and patient volumes must be built out for each revenue-generating department, such as the emergency department, labor and delivery, operating room, radiology, lab, intensive care, catheterization laboratory, medical and surgical floors, and so on. The costs of nonpatient care departments and overhead must also be figured into the equation, including laundry and linen, supplies, housekeeping, food and dietary, patient transport, security, administration, admitting, facilities and engineering, parking, risk management, and so on. Such an analysis is complex and time-consuming, but critical.

Some cost-benefit analyses are challenging because the financial connection between a particular recommendation and its intended benefit is somewhat imprecise. For instance, calculating the cost-benefit of hiring a public relations, lobbying, or leadership training firm may be difficult since the intended benefits are not fully known or quantifiable. Therefore, other benefits may need to come into play to justify the costs.

Because cost-benefit projections are often based on estimates and assumptions, they should be conservative to account for any unforeseen events that could alter expected returns. For instance, volume projections can fluctuate in particular geographic regions based on the rise or fall of local economic conditions. Competitors may unexpectedly merge, creating a well-funded company that could impact revenue. Changing government regulations and new tax laws can suddenly cut into projected profits.

It is important to note that while some stellar recommendations can generate a ten-fold or higher ROI, most don't. In cases where internal performance improvement teams or external consulting firms propose huge ROIs on particular recommendations, I have learned to take a very conservative position when evaluating them. A prominent consultant once told me that on such recommendations, he cuts the ROI down to one-third of the original projection. Too often, ROIs are overstated and reflect the best possible outcomes.

Jumping the Gun

One of the most common mistakes made during Step 5 is making recommendations before completing the necessary due diligence of thorough scrutiny and analysis. Because there can be a sense of excitement after identifying a seemingly fabulous solution to an operational problem, it is tempting to propose the recommendation prematurely. Recommendations proposed prematurely stand a good chance of either getting blocked by senior leadership, who shoot holes through them, or failing after they are implemented.

In either case, credibility is destroyed. Worse, however, are the sunk costs and resources that go into implementing poor recommendations. Failed large-scale implementations can even damage the viability of an organization or have long-lasting effects of distrust on the part of impacted employees and customers. In the end, leadership takes the blame.

Seasoned consultants are cautious and perform the required research and due diligence before they propose any recommendation. In addition, as mentioned above, when recommendations are proposed, seasoned consultants will intentionally write "DRAFT" on the top of the *Recommendations Report*. This gives others one last chance to review and modify recommendations before they are approved and implemented, further increasing their chances for success.

I want to drive this point home a little more: never submit a recommendation in the midst of excitement or an emotional high when the due diligence has not been completed. Remain poised and complete the required research in order to fully vet the recommendation. Comparatively, this is one of the biggest reasons so many new businesses fail. An entrepreneur hasn't completed the required research and homework before refinancing his or her home to open a pizza place or yogurt shop. Overly excited entrepreneurs get a new business idea and then move enthusiastically forward without the necessary information and skills to make it successful. They haven't reduced the risk factors by conducting a sufficient competitive assessment, performing the required market research, or completing critical financial analyses.

Entrepreneurship is often mistakenly perceived as being all about taking risk. That is not true. Entrepreneurship is all about doing adequate research and homework and acquiring the relevant skills to be successful. There are no shortcuts to excellent outcomes. Ask any great athlete who has paid the price; there are no shortcuts. Luck can certainly be a factor. For instance, if the best sprinter in the world pulls a hamstring during a race, the second-best sprinter wins the prize. But luck is the exception to the rule. The rule is doing the required work that helps guarantee the outcome. When I started Kodiak Cakes, I felt confident that our company products could successfully compete in the market, because I had completed the rigorous consumer and competitive research to minimize the risks. Improving an operation with thoroughly vetted recommendations is no different.

Completing the Rembrandt

Once the effort has been made in proposing the right recommendations, it is like putting the final brushstrokes on a masterpiece. The required research, benchmarking, and recommendations have been completed. There is a feeling of perfection and pride in a job well done.

Once finished, the masterpiece, or in this case, the *Recommendations Report*, is given to the decision makers to approve and move on to implementation. The Rembrandt is complete.

CHAPTER SUMMARY: Key Points

1. Step 5 to optimizing performance is recommending the right operational solutions to the problems and opportunities identified in Step 3. Plan on dedicating approximately ten percent of an operational improvement project to this step.

2. The objective of Step 5 is to achieve the performance targets identified in Step 2.

3. The first step in determining the best operational improvements to recommend is reviewing the operational problems and opportunities listed in the *Findings Report* from Step 3. The potential solutions identified in Steps 3 and 4 are then evaluated. Further study and brainstorming may be necessary to determine the right solutions.

4. Recommendations are then listed on a *Recommendations Report*, which outlines the operational problems and opportunities and their corresponding improvement recommendations.

5. Recommendations listed on the *Recommendations Report* should include supportive information and data to endorse them, such as benchmarking information, cost-benefit analyses, financial projections and proformas, and side-by-side comparisons between an operation's current and proposed states.

6. Improvement recommendations should be written as specifically as possible, whereas, general recommendations lack specific details on what is to be implemented.

7. One of the most common mistakes is proposing recommendations before completing the required due diligence of scrutiny and evaluation for each recommendation.

8. The *Recommendations Report* should be put in "DRAFT" format to allow leaders, experts, and key stakeholders the chance to review and modify the recommendations before they are finalized.

9. A final *Recommendations Report* becomes the key document that decision makers review in order to approve the implementation of specific performance improvement recommendations.

STEP 6

Implement Recommendations

PHASE I. ASSESSMENT
Stage I - Opportunity Analysis
Step 1: Measure current performance
Step 2: Establish performance targets
Stage II - Operational Review
Step 3: Evaluate underperforming operations
Step 4: Benchmark best practice organizations
PHASE II. IMPLEMENTATION
Stage III - Recommendations & implementation
Step 5: Recommend operational improvements
Step 6: Implement recommendations
Stage IV - Sustainability & Refinement
Step 7: Monitor outcomes
Step 8: Refine improvements

Step 6 to optimizing performance is implementing the performance improvement recommendations listed in the *Recommendations Report* of Step 5 in the most efficient and effective manner possible. Plan on devoting approximately twenty-five percent of your improvement project to this step. Successfully implementing the right recommendations comes down to proper execution.

It is interesting that professional athletes and coaches frequently lament during post-game interviews, "We needed to execute better." A professional football team may have a great play in the playbook, but unless they can execute it, the play fails. Likewise, I have seen performance improvement implementations fail because they were not properly executed.

Successful implementations are based on the proper execution of two fundamentals: (1) project management and (2) change management. Project management is the effective supervision and controlled oversight of completing an improvement initiative according to an organized plan. Change management is the ability to lead and facilitate change within an organization given the human and psychological variables, such as vulnerability, fear, fatigue, distress, and resistance. Project management and change management go hand in hand. Both must be properly and concurrently executed for an implementation to succeed.

In practice, some organizations give full credence to proper project management techniques. For instance, they set up a well-functioning transformation project management office with a steering committee, team leaders, project teams, project management software, etc., but they neglect the often weightier, human component of change management. As a result, complex or sensitive implementations are less successful than they could have been, because the human aspects were undervalued.

I recall a senior administrator who decided to replace the director of a department—a fairly simple task, operationally speaking. However, when the administrator disclosed his plan to replace the director, the entire department was so upset that they threatened to resign and walk out. The administrator had entirely overlooked the human component of his recommendation. As a result, his plan failed.

Because effective project management and change management are so critical to a performance improvement initiative, extensive research and literature have been devoted to these subjects. In addition, there are consulting and management training firms that specialize in these disciplines. Such firms provide consulting services, expensive training seminars, and professional certification programs for organizations. Universities throughout the world offer courses on these two subjects. Many organizations regularly develop their own internal management training programs and host guest speakers who present leadership development seminars on these topics.

Rather than redundantly writing on the proper principles and tools of project management and change management, this chapter addresses only a few of the most critical components. In my experience, these particular components become the Achilles' heel of this step if applied improperly. Yet, if applied properly, they help guarantee an implementation's success.

Project Management

Classical project management theory advocates the use of project charters, issue logs, risk planning, implementation teams, steering committees, project sponsors, project managers, project budgeting, communications plans, effective meetings, Gantt charts, project management software, project plans, closing a project, and many other principles, tools, roles, and functions. While many of the elements in this overly exhaustive list are integral and contribute to a project's success, three of them are crucial and seem to frequently falter. These three crucial elements are: (1) the project sponsor; (2) the project manager; and (3) the project plan.

➤ **The Project Sponsor.** The project sponsor is an executive within the organization who authorizes, supports, and oversees the project. During the implementation step, this role is perhaps the most vital because recommendations can rarely be implemented effectively without the complete backing and support of a high-level project sponsor. The resistance to change can be so strong that an organization will withstand any other person, team, or stakeholder trying to initiate change. The authority and position to initiate change must be ever-present. In addition to ensuring a full and complete implementation, fortitude must be a predominant characteristic of the one holding the authority. Any perceived weakness or hesitancy in the project sponsor's ability to back the project and take it to completion can compromise its success. The project sponsor must stand steadfast and resolute through all imminent and opposing forces.

➤ **The Project Manager.** The project manager, or project director (depending on the size and scope of the project), is responsible for developing the overall project plan and establishing and managing various teams responsible for implementation. An effective project manager employs the necessary tools and elements of good project management in the most efficient manner possible. The goal and responsibilities of the project manager are to implement a set of recommendations as effectively and efficiently as possible.

I recall an experience in which a certified project manager was hired to lead a multimillion-dollar implementation project. While this person was knowledgeable about project management, he got so absorbed in the details of project management protocol that he was unable to execute and implement. Consequently, time lapsed while nothing was accomplished, and he had to be replaced.

Effective project managers have a clear vision of what needs to be accomplished and the intuition of how to implement efficiently. They can also identify the right project management tools and employ them in the simplest manner. They are organized, know how to select high-performing teams, hold people accountable to their assignments, are sensitive to cultural issues, show tenacity when confronting opposition, are prudent with finances and budgets, and reach milestones on time. They are prepared, detail-oriented, competent leaders, and understand change management principles. They know how to delegate, follow up, present succinct updates, and execute.

With such a list of qualifications, do these people exist? Absolutely. They are pulled from the pool of high-performing, driven, and conscientious staff of an organization. Although their knowledge base may differ from that of certain subject matter experts, they know how to leverage others' expertise, like a quarterback throwing the ball to a wide receiver or handing off to a fullback. Excellent project managers are task-oriented and get things done.

➤ **The Project Plan.** The project plan is a high-level implementation plan that lists each recommendation, prioritizes them, identifies team leaders and teams responsible for implementation, and specifies the project start and estimated completion dates. Project plans should also contain a project description field and the intended deliverable, if not clearly identified in the recommendation field. In addition, other pertinent information, such as each recommendation's associated implementation costs and financial opportunity, should be shown. The project plan must be succinct and simple, not cumbersome. Unfortunately, many project managers include too much detailed information and use overly complicated project management software to maintain them. However, while sophisticated project management programs may be necessary for complicated projects, such as a software installation project, a simple spreadsheet is usually sufficient.

Once the project plan is finalized, the project manager uses it to make assignments and commence the project. After the project has begun, the project plan turns into a status report showing the implementation progress as well as updates for each recommendation. At this point, a few other key information fields are also used in the project plan, such as "status," "update," and "next steps." The "status" field indicates at a glance whether each recommendation is on schedule. This particular field contains a few key words such as "on track" and can also be highlighted in green, yellow, or red, like a traffic light. The "status" field is highlighted in green if the project is on track. Yellow highlighting means the recommendation is meeting some barriers. If the project is critically off track and meeting serious obstacles, red highlighting would indicate that rapid intervention is necessary. An "update" field provides specific notes and information about the status of each recommendation. The "next steps" field specifies what is to be accomplished in the near future, by whom, and when. A succinct project plan template is provided in Figure 17.

	A	B	C	D	E
1	**Recommendations**	**Description & Deliverable**	**Start Date**	**Est. Completion Date**	**Status**
2	**Recommendation #1**				
3	**Recommendation #2**				
4	**Recommendation #3**				
5	**Recommendation #4**				
6	**Recommendation #5**				
7	**Total**				

	F	G	H	I	J	K
1	**Update**	**Next Steps**	**Implement-ation Costs**	**Opportunity**	**Team Leader**	**Team**
2						
3						
4						
5						
6						
7			**$ 0.00**	**$ 0.00**		

Figure 17: **Project plan template**

The project plan thus becomes the project manager's primary tool, not only to initiate the project but also to track and govern its progress through completion. The project plan must provide enough information so that a simple but accurate summary of the entire project can be easily reviewed by senior leadership and a steering committee. The costs and financial opportunities are also tracked in the report and totaled at the bottom. This provides an economic picture of the entire project at any given time and helps control costs while ensuring the projected return on investment is realized.

Each individual responsible for implementing specific recommendations should provide weekly updates to the project manager. The project manager then updates the project plan. The updates should include accrued expenditures and ROI information. The project plan then becomes the key instrument of the project's overall status, which goes to administration or a steering committee for review.

For large and complex projects, the project manager actually becomes the project director, overseeing a master project plan. Each individual responsible for implementing specific recommendations or sets of recommendations becomes a project manager, rather than a team leader. Each project manager then has their own separate project or work plan and implementation team, depending on the size of the project.

A work plan is similar to a project plan but provides more detail by breaking down particular recommendations into specific implementation tasks and subtasks. Each task and subtask is prioritized with its own start and completion dates and shows the project manager or team leader, team, implementation costs, financial opportunity, status, update, and next steps fields. On the other hand, a project plan is higher-level and keeps track of the status of each recommendation without going into the detail required to implement each recommendation. Figure 18 depicts the tasks and subtasks for a particular recommendation on a work plan.

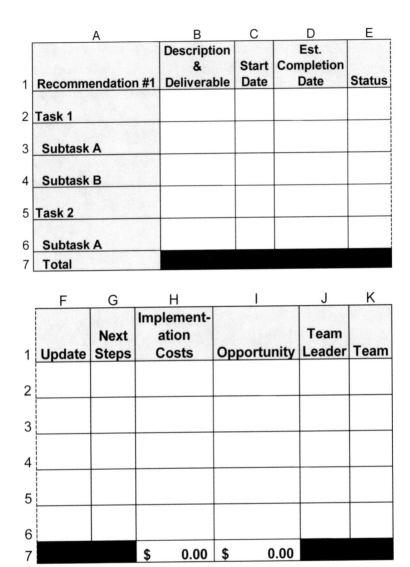

Figure 18: **Work plan template**

Those responsible for implementing specific recommendations manage and update their own project plans. To illustrate, suppose you recommend implementing an ERP (Enterprise Resource Planning) computer system with different modules for several different departments such as manufacturing, order entry, purchasing, finance, accounting, and human resources. The overall project is so vast that it requires a project director to develop and control the plan. Individual project managers oversee each department module by managing their individual projects or work plans. They also regularly coordinate with the project director so she can ensure that the entire project is progressing according to preset timelines, contingencies, and budgeted costs.

Change Management

Organizations commonly make three fatal errors when managing change inherent in an operations improvement project: (1) failing to designate strong, supportive senior leadership, (2) failing to maintain the thrust of the project through completion, and (3) not sustaining the improvements after completing the implementation. Each of these is addressed below.

➢ **Supportive Leadership**: In addition to the essential role of the strong executive project sponsor, an organization must also uphold the implementation step with its entire senior leadership staff, particularly the CEO. Otherwise, despite the efforts of a strong sponsor, the project can face great opposition and risk failure. I have witnessed countless times in which senior executive leaders give lip service to backing a project, but when implementation comes to their respective areas, they back down. In turn, the department directors who are not pressed to support the project follow suit and oppose changes in their departments as well. Without complete commitment by all senior leadership, trying to implement change can be like entering a den of territorial lions who will eat you alive when you enter their area. Sooner or later, the project sponsor, unfortunately, concedes and implements change only in the areas that support it. As a result, operational outcomes fall short of targeted performance levels. Unfortunately, this lack of leadership backing is so commonplace that it becomes a primary reason for performance improvement failure. Therefore, it is critical that the entire administrative team be totally committed to project implementation.

When an administrative team is thus committed, and they mandate the same commitment from their management staff, implementation is profoundly easier, and the project sponsor and project managers are more effective. In fact, the success of a project often hinges on a simple mandate given by the CEO to his or her leadership team, requiring them to fully and proactively support an implementation effort. At one organization where I consulted, the CEO routinely issued a formal letter to his vice presidents, directors, and managers, expecting their full support and cooperation prior to each improvement project. This letter eliminated many potential conflicts between the project sponsor and departments involved in change.

Dr. Timothy R. Clark, in his breakthrough book, *Epic Change: How to Lead Change in the Global Age* (Wiley/Jossey-Bass, 2008), refers to this crucial component of change management as "establishing a coalition of leaders." Without a leadership coalition firmly resolved to execute and implement recommendations, the overall project is destined to achieve only partial success, if not complete failure. The leadership coalition must be in place before initiating implementation.

➢ **Project Completion**: Some implementation projects are so complex and enormous that project managers, steering committees, implementation teams, management, and staff can burn out midway through the project. During the period of exhaustion and fatigue, individuals experience difficulty trying to stay focused on the project. Other improvement projects and priorities begin to surface, distracting their attention from the project. At this point, essential staff becomes less and less engaged, and the project never realizes full implementation.

At one organization I worked for, we undertook a four-year implementation project to reduce operating costs. I was the project director over the project. After two and a half years of aggressively installing several large computer systems, implementing expensive automated equipment, and engaging a number of consulting firms to assist with different aspects of the project, project managers and teams began to hit the wall of fatigue. As their energy diminished, they grew weary, thin-skinned, and emotional. Some even got sick. Others just backed off the project and stopped attending meetings. The prolonged stress and mental and physical exhaustion were unhealthy and caused many to retreat. In such a tremendously arduous implementation, energy levels, endurance, and proper staffing must be considered and addressed before commencing the project.

In *Epic Change*, Dr. Clark also discusses this aspect of change management. He asserts that any change project requires individuals to devote more incremental energy to implementing change than the baseline energy required to run current operations. During implementation, staff members are expected to do more work than their regular positions originally demanded. Where does the incremental energy come from, and how long can it be sustained before it must be replenished?

If the energy is not consistently replenished, people begin to naturally check out of the project or leave the organization altogether because they simply cannot continue. The great economist Herbert Stein captured this principle with his famous aphorism: "If something cannot go on forever, it will stop." Or said another way, "That which is unsustainable cannot be sustained and surely must end." Carrying out a change project entails recharging the batteries of those carrying out the changes.

This crucial factor must be incorporated throughout each of the eight steps of performance improvement and operational excellence initiatives. There are several key ways to refuel the energy of the people engaged in a change initiative, as detailed in Dr. Clark's book. But it is up to the leadership coalition, project sponsor, and project manager to understand this factor beforehand and ensure that those amplifying their efforts and energy for the project are supported, backed, encouraged, and assisted in order to complete the project. They must have balance, rest, relief, incentives, time off, recognition, motivation, and most especially see results, to avoid prolonged distress and imminent psychological and physical fatigue.

➤ **Sustainability**: Once recommendations are implemented, organizations seem to suddenly and habitually back off the project and divert their attention elsewhere. As this abrupt withdrawal occurs, operational changes begin to revert to their former state, and many improvements are lost. It's the same as removing braces from newly set teeth without wearing a retainer and then watching the teeth shift back to their original position.

To whatever degree leadership turns its attention away from a project after implementation, a corresponding return to the old status quo should be anticipated. To make permanent change, leaders must continue surveying their implemented recommendations to ensure they do not alter. From a change management perspective, this is accomplished as leaders continuously monitor each implementation to ensure their hard-won improvements remain intact.

In some cases, improvements must be regularly reviewed for an additional one, two, or even three years. This simple review and oversight must be performed after implementation, as it is a tenuous time during which the elasticity of an improved operation must be controlled. For example, after a department is reorganized to fulfill an improvement recommendation, it is common for the new director of the department to make additional organizational changes. However, these additional changes usually negatively affect operational outcomes, and the department reverts to past practices. Because sustainability is so crucial, I will address it further in Steps 7 and 8.

CHAPTER SUMMARY: Key Points

1. Step 6 to optimizing performance is implementing performance improvement recommendations in the most efficient and effective manner possible. Plan on devoting about twenty-five percent of an improvement project to this step.

2. Successfully implementing the right recommendations is based on the proper execution of two fundamentals: (1) project management and (2) change management.

3. Project management is the effective supervision and controlled oversight of completing an improvement initiative according to an organized plan.

4. Change management is the ability to lead and facilitate change within an organization, given the human and psychological variables often associated with vulnerability, fear, fatigue, distress, and resistance.

5. Three crucial components of project management are:

   - **The Project Sponsor**: The project sponsor is the executive within the organization who authorizes, supports, and oversees the project. This role is vital because recommendations cannot be implemented effectively without the complete backing and support of a project sponsor.

   - **The Project Manager**: The project manager, or project director (depending on the size and scope of the project), is in charge of developing the overall project plan and for establishing and managing the various teams responsible for implementation. An effective project manager implements the recommendations as effectively and efficiently as possible.

- **The Project Plan**: The project plan is a high-level implementation plan that lists all recommendations, prioritizes them, and identifies the person and team responsible for implementation. It also contains completion dates, project costs, a return on investment, and other pertinent information. Once the project plan is finalized and underway, it becomes a status report for tracking progress.

6. Three crucial components of change management are:

- **Supportive Leadership**: All change initiatives must be firmly supported and backed by the entire senior leadership team. Without this leadership coalition, resistance to change can be so strong that implementation efforts fail.

- **Project Completion**: Some implementation projects are so complex and enormous that leadership and staff begin to burn out before the project is complete. To combat fatigue and ensure a project is taken to completion, the increased energy that staff expends to implement change must be replenished throughout the project.

- **Sustainability**: Once the implementation step is complete, leadership cannot afford to withdraw their oversight over newly implemented recommendations. Without continued oversight, operational changes regress, and many improvements are lost.

STEP 7

Monitor Outcomes

PHASE I. ASSESSMENT
Stage I - Opportunity Analysis
Step 1: Measure current performance
Step 2: Establish performance targets
Stage II - Operational Review
Step 3: Evaluate underperforming operations
Step 4: Benchmark best practice organizations
PHASE II. IMPLEMENTATION
Stage III - Recommendations & implementation
Step 5: Recommend operational improvements
Step 6: Implement recommendations
Stage IV - Sustainability & Refinement
Step 7: Monitor outcomes
Step 8: Refine improvements

S tep 7 is monitoring outcomes to ensure performance targets are attained and sustained. Devote approximately five percent of an improvement project to this step. Step 7 is the simplest step, but it is of paramount importance. This is because the entire purpose of a performance improvement project is to increase an operation's current outputs, outcomes, or deliverables to the elevated performance targets established during Step 2. Step 7 is directed at monitoring the KPI dashboards developed in Step 1 to ensure the implemented recommendations produce the targeted results. A performance improvement project isn't complete upon implementation but rather when targeted outcomes are attained and sustained. Even then, we might say performance improvement never ends because, as organizations progress, higher performance targets are set, operations are again refined, and KPIs are monitored to ensure new targets are met. It is an ongoing cycle.

Once recommendations are implemented in Step 6, the new operational results should be reflected on KPI dashboards. In some cases, results are immediate, while in other cases, results may experience some time lag. For instance, implementing a new piece of automated equipment may yield immediate results, while implementing new incentives for a sales department may experience a delay before revenues increase. However, after a reasonable amount of time has elapsed, depending on the improvements made, KPIs should reflect the expected operational outcomes. If KPIs show that targeted performance levels have been reached and sustained over time, the improvement project was successful. If, however, performance targets were not reached, or if they were reached for only a short duration before declining, the project needs further refinement, which will be discussed in Step 8.

With successful performance improvement projects in which targets are reached and sustained, leaders must never stop monitoring KPI dashboards. When leaders quit monitoring dashboards, they remove accountability and the expectation of high performance from their employees. When this occurs, they also remove much of the incentive and drive to sustain new results. Employees feel they can then relax. But they can't. Faithfully monitoring KPIs after implementation is the key to ensuring sustained improvements.

If KPIs are consistently monitored and performance begins to decline, unforeseen factors may be impacting operations. Weakening economic conditions or greater competition can reduce sales, which in turn causes underutilization of a manufacturing operation. When underutilization occurs, production volumes decline while fixed costs (e.g., administration, marketing, and overhead costs) can remain high.

This means the cost per unit rises as fewer units must now absorb all the fixed costs. For example, if production volumes decrease from 100,000 to 50,000 units, and fixed costs remain at $10 million, the fixed cost per unit will increase from $100 ($10 million / 100,000) to $200 ($10 million / 50,000). In such a case, the operation needs immediate refinement by referring to Step 8, Refine Improvements, because the costs are too high to sustain with fewer units being produced. Fortunately, KPIs will alert leadership to a negative trend in the early stages, allowing leadership to promptly respond.

Inversely, unforeseen factors can positively affect performance, such as an economic boom that causes performance targets to be exceeded. On these occasions, performance targets should be raised to new levels. Further operational refinements, discussed in Step 8, can then be made to adjust to new customer demand levels and higher performance targets.

CHAPTER SUMMARY: Key Points

1. Step 7 to optimizing performance is monitoring outcomes to ensure performance targets are attained and sustained. Approximately, five percent of an improvement project is devoted to this step.

2. While Step 7 is perhaps the easiest, it is nonetheless essential because it determines whether project implementations were successful and if they achieved and maintained performance targets.

3. When performance targets are not reached, or if they are reached for only a short time before declining, the project needs further refinement.

4. Monitoring KPIs after implementation is an ongoing process and essential for sustaining results.

5. Unforeseen internal and external factors may negatively impact future performance, causing the need for operational refinement. On the flip side, unforeseen factors may positively affect performance, requiring leaders to raise performance targets and make operational refinements to reach the new targets.

STEP 8

Refine Improvements

PHASE I. ASSESSMENT
Stage I - Opportunity Analysis
Step 1: Measure current performance
Step 2: Establish performance targets
Stage II - Operational Review
Step 3: Evaluate underperforming operations
Step 4: Benchmark best practice organizations
PHASE II. IMPLEMENTATION
Stage III - Recommendations & implementation
Step 5: Recommend operational improvements
Step 6: Implement recommendations
Stage IV - Sustainability & Refinement
Step 7: Monitor outcomes
Step 8: Refine improvements

Step 8 to optimizing performance is refining the implemented improvements as necessary to achieve targeted outcomes. Because this step never goes away, the relative weight of time devoted to it is higher than Step 7. As such, you will devote approximately ten percent of an improvement project to this step because of its long-term nature.

If the improvements implemented in Step 6 do not attain and sustain targeted performance levels, as indicated in Step 7, they must be refined. Making refinements is expected, as it is nearly impossible to implement every recommendation perfectly. Making refinements is like playing chess. After moving a chess piece during a particular turn, you may need to modify the move on your next turn, depending on your opponent's move.

Some refinements are simple, while others are more arduous. For instance, while on a consulting engagement for a large organization, I directed the restructuring of the entire management layer for several departments. The restructuring consisted of eliminating more than fifty positions and then replacing them with fewer than forty new positions. After reorganizing the management layer and rehiring the new positions, performance still waned in certain areas.

As our consulting team set out to refine the implementation, we realized a few of the newly created positions needed to be elevated to higher management levels, and that we hired the wrong leaders in a couple of positions. Although we did the best we could, the implementation wasn't perfect. However, after refinements were made, the newly organized departments achieved the desired outcomes in every area. In hindsight, our implementation effort proved to be about ninety to ninety-five percent correct, while refinements accounted for the other five to ten percent.

On a larger scale, multimillion-dollar computer systems are regularly installed in organizations to produce efficient, automated processes. Such an immense implementation is certain to experience difficulties after its go-live date. In fact, organizations expect problems to occur and prepare for the go-live date with excessive IT personnel stationed in every department to make adjustments to the system as necessary.

As obstacles occur after recommendations are implemented, it is usually apparent where refinements need to be made. For instance, if a new piece of manufacturing equipment is installed but does not function properly, it is usually easy to identify defects in the piece of equipment. In other cases, problems may be much more elusive. In these cases, KPIs must be carefully scrutinized at each operational level until the issues are isolated. This top-down analysis, discussed in Step 2, showed that while KPIs at the organizational level may indicate overall problems and opportunities, KPIs at the division, business unit, department, function, and work-task levels must be reviewed to identify and isolate the specific problems and opportunities.

Once you have identified problems, refinements are usually made in one of four ways.

- First, improvements may need to be refined, abandoned, or replaced with better solutions. For example, a newly installed piece of manufacturing equipment that is not working properly at the outset may just need simple refinements. However, a newly installed computer system that simply does not work as intended may need to be abandoned or replaced with a different solution. I've witnessed both.

- Second, some problems and opportunities may have been overlooked during the operational review step. In these circumstances, additional solutions will need to be developed and implemented. A closer look at an operation that is still not meeting performance targets may reveal that employees are underproducing and quitting because compensation is too low. This problem may have been overlooked during the operational review process.

- Third, if an operation appears to be functioning well but targets are still not being reached, it is possible that the targets were set unreasonably high and need to be adjusted. Because performance targets are estimated based on internal and external benchmarks, historical data, and projections, they could still be slightly off. For instance, setting a performance target to increase net operating income by $12 million during the next fiscal year may have been unrealistic and should be adjusted down to $10 million.

- Fourth, even if an operation appears to be functioning properly and the targets are appropriate, other unanticipated factors may be influencing the targets. A sudden surge in fuel costs could be eroding operating margins. In these cases, either new solutions must be identified and implemented or performance targets must be readjusted—or both.

As mentioned in Step 7, unforeseen factors can actually elevate performance to exceed targets. If a competitor went out of business, for example, sales would likely increase. When an organization has the ability to exceed its targets, it should set new targets. As organizations naturally progress and new business objectives (i.e., the strategy, missions, visions, goals, and values) evolve, performance targets should be simultaneously adjusted to meet new demands. As targets change, operations must be refined so outcomes, outputs, or deliverables continually achieve or exceed performance expectations.

Refining improvements becomes the capstone principle to optimizing performance, where the cycle of progression never ends. Objectives are established, operational performance is optimized to achieve those objectives, and new objectives are established and pursued in an effort to achieve a continuous cycle of advancement.

CHAPTER SUMMARY: Key Points

1. Step 8 to optimizing performance is refining the implemented improvements as needed in order to realize targeted outcomes. You will devote approximately ten percent of an improvement project to this step.

2. Implemented recommendations that are not achieving performance targets must be refined so performance targets can be met.

3. It is nearly impossible to implement all recommendations perfectly. Expect to make some operational refinements.

4. While it is usually easy to locate the area of an operation that needs refinement, a top-down analysis of KPIs at each operational level may be required.

5. If targets are not being met after improvement recommendations have been implemented, refinements are typically made in one of four ways:

   • Recommendations that were implemented but are still not achieving performance targets may need to be refined, abandoned, or replaced with alternative solutions.

   • If some problems and opportunities were missed during Step 3, Evaluate Underperforming Operations, new corresponding solutions will need to be developed and implemented.

   • If operations are not reaching performance targets, it is possible that the targets need to be adjusted.

- Unforeseen external factors that are causing targets to not be reached may need to be addressed.

6. As organizations progress over time and their business objectives evolve, performance targets and operations need to be adjusted to meet new demands and goals.

7. The capstone principle to optimizing performance is perpetuating a cycle of progress that never ends. Performance targets are established, operations are improved to reach those targets, and higher targets are set and reached in an effort to achieve a continuous cycle of forward progress.

SUMMARY OF STEPS

The eight steps of the *Managing in Reverse* methodology are listed below. Figure 19 summarizes these steps in a table showing the corresponding four stages and two phases, as well as the relative weights of time typically devoted to each. A graphical representation of these relative weights is shown in Figures 20 and 21, respectively.

Step 1: Measure the current performance of an operation's outputs, outcomes, or deliverables.

Step 2: Establish performance targets for the outputs, outcomes, or deliverables of an operation and calculate the improvement opportunity.

Step 3: Evaluate underperforming operations to identify specific problems and opportunities for improvement.

Step 4: Benchmark best practice organizations to help determine solutions and improvement recommendations.

Step 5: Recommend the right operational solutions to improve problems and realize opportunities.

Step 6: Implement performance improvement recommendations efficiently and effectively.

Step 7: Monitor outcomes to ensure performance targets are attained and sustained.

Step 8: Refine the implemented improvements to achieve targeted outcomes.

	Relative Weight
PHASE I. ASSESSMENT	**50%**
Stage I - Opportunity Analysis	*15%*
Step 1: Measure current performance	10%
Step 2: Establish performance targets	5%
Stage II - Operational Review	*35%*
Step 3: Evaluate underperforming operations	25%
Step 4: Benchmark best practice organizations	10%
PHASE II. IMPLEMENTATION	**50%**
Stage III - Recommendations & implementation	*35%*
Step 5: Recommend operational improvements	10%
Step 6: Implement recommendations	25%
Stage IV - Sustainability & Refinement	*15%*
Step 7: Monitor outcomes	5%
Step 8: Refine improvements	10%

Figure 19: **Relative amounts of time devoted to each phase, stage, and step**

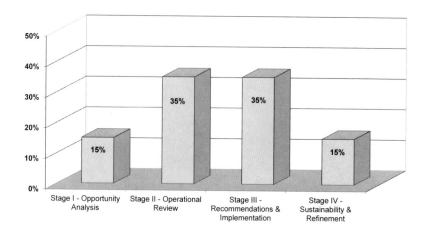

Figure 20: **Relative percent of time dedicated to each stage, graphically illustrated**

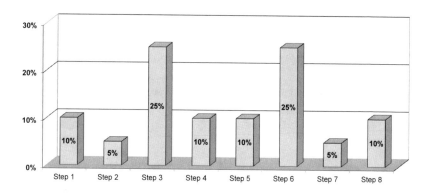

Figure 21: **Relative percent of time dedicated to each step graphically illustrated**

ABOUT THE AUTHOR

For decades, Jonathan Clark has helped some of the finest organizations in the US improve their performance and operational outcomes. He is a former vice president of a Fortune 100 Company, vice president of a Fortune 500 Company, and hospital system associate administrator. Mr. Clark is also the founder of Kodiak Cakes. He obtained his BS in accounting and his MBA from the University of Utah as a Dean's Scholar.